BOWLED OVER ...
AND OUT!

BOWLED OVER ...
AND OUT!

Nigel Chapman

David
Happy memories of SF days
with best wishes
Nigel

CHARLCOMBE BOOKS

Charlcombe Books
17 George's Road, Bath BA1 6EY
tel: 01225-335813

First published 2011

ISBN: 978 0 9568510 1 7

Printed and bound in Great Britain by
Midway Colour Print, Trowbridge, Wiltshire

Contents

	Foreword	7
1	Elysian Fields	9
2	Home	20
3	Halcyon Days	28
4	Lord's	37
5	Essex	49
6	The Robins	59
7	Coaches ... Coaching	67
8	North Oxford	75
9	Oxfordshire	83
10	Rural Joys	90
11	Cape Town	104
12	Over and Out	113

To my Dad
who taught me that cricket should be played for fun

This book has only been made possible through the help of a lot of friends. I am indebted to Stephen Cox, for the loan of 'Cricketer' magazines from the 1960s and '70s; to Martin Foster, who kindly read through the first drafts of each chapter and made many sensible suggestions; to Michael Morrogh at Shrewsbury, who delved into their archives to find the details of the 1999 tour of Cape Town; to Felix Beardmore-Gray who provided the scorecard of the final Arabs' Match as well as the photo of cricket at Horris Hill; to Christopher Dawkins for providing a whole selection of pictures from the Felsted archives; to Chris Nathan, the archivist at St. Edward's, Oxford, for the photo of Brian Edrich; to Charles Churchill for his superb composition of James Weaver being 'out first ball', taken at Summer Fields in 1982, which adorns the cover; to John Mayall who in his final days nobly read the finished version and made several corrections and useful suggestions.

In particular, I thank Johnny Barclay not just for his kind and flattering foreword but also for putting me in touch with Stephen Chalke whose encouragement, guidance and expertise made a fanciful idea a reality.

The stories here are as I remember them, more or less, though one or two names have had to be changed!

Nigel Chapman
April 2011

Foreword
by John Barclay

Nigel Chapman was a great teacher and I'll tell you why. Although he never actually taught me anything academic, he did teach me cricket. And that really mattered, at least it did to me. To us boys he was still very young and had style. It was his cover drive in the nets that did the trick. Quick feet and hands, eyes on the ball and whack! I loved that.

Example and minor heroism are a rich combination but, above all, Nigel (Mr Chapman to me) was a motivator. On away matches he would travel on the bus with an abundance of sweets which were awarded for moments of triumph on the field. One sweet for every wicket taken or catch caught, a packet for 5 wickets or 20 runs, half a packet for 10 runs and the rest shared out amongst the majority who had a lousy match. The sweets were dished out on the bus going home which put paid to the singing and general merriment in the back. Ten green bottles and one man went to mow begin to wear a little thin after a while.

Cricket was all very well. I confess I did well in the sweets department. Cricket was my strength. Rugby was quite a different kettle of fish. Chappers (we called him that too) liked rugby. One day we travelled to Cheam down in the Horris Hill direction for the Prep Schools Sevens Tournament. I was Summer Fields' scrum half and small. It was all very well playing against feeble opposition but when we encountered Cheam it was a very different matter. They had recruited two enormous overseas players from the East (Siam, I think) to beef up their scrum. We were no match for them. I was flattened, squashed and mauled by large, trampling, metal studded rugby boots. I hated it. Fingers are so vulnerable.

We didn't win the tournament. I did not travel back in the bus but instead in the front seat of Chappers' green van in which I was less likely to be sick. No sweets this time; rugby football was not my cup of tea.

Chappers used a rich trio of enthusiasm, energy and encouragement to get the best out of boys. He would love to have played first-class cricket himself and, who knows, perhaps even for England but my guess is that his talent would have been wasted. His love of cricket and sport made him a great teacher whose influence upon the young (me and many others) has been priceless.

1. ELYSIAN FIELDS

Of course, the sun always shone in those days. Life was innocent and carefree. And the cricket was glorious.

We were so lucky with our mentor, Mr Eardley. EWE (we called him eewee because of his initials) was a deputy headmaster, head of classics and English, but most important of all, master i/c cricket. And we loved him, but he certainly loved us more, especially if we played cricket.

"Will you give me a net today, Sir, please?"

"Sorry, Chippo, I've promised I'd take Jules this break, but it'd be a great help if you could come and bowl at him as he needs some practice against spin."

And so it happened day in, day out. Every spare moment EWE would take one of us to the nets, with a clutch of bowlers to add spice to the occasion. Not that we'd do that much bowling as after a couple of minutes he'd spot a technical problem and then chuck balls endlessly at the batsman to iron out that particular weakness, while we ran around like monkeys picking up the balls and handing them back to him. It was fun and painless as you well knew that tomorrow, or the next day, you'd get all the attention as the batsman.

I'm sure he thought we were quite good, but he never let on. There was Jules, the Captain, a reliable opening bat; Welly was the tall frightening opening bowler who liked a slog in the middle order; Dicko, always buzzing around and chatting, kept wicket; I bowled leg-spin and batted a bit; and HW, whose Dad played for Suffolk, was at 11 just a bit younger but fielded brilliantly and scored useful runs. For most of us it was the third year in the 1st XI, and I think EWE had been building this team for a special season. And, of course, the sun always shone in those days.

But on the day it really mattered, it didn't. We were playing Grimwade House away and it was damp and dour. I suppose the match could have been called off but that wasn't the way to do things – some sawdust, a towel and a sweater or two and we'd cope.

It all went wrong from the start. We lost the toss and had to field in a fine drizzle. No-one seemed able to bowl properly and Grimwade rattled up 101 for only a few wickets. Our batting was equally lacklustre and we were bowled out for a pitiful 33 with some twenty minutes to spare.

We returned somewhat forlorn, but not that dispirited. Sid, the HM, met the bus as we were getting off and commiserated as we waited to collect our kit. Finally EWE emerged.

"What on earth happened?" said Sid.

"I don't know. I just don't know." There was an air of gloom about him as the words choked out. It was then that we boys realised how much we'd let him down – we could and should have been his first unbeaten team.

For the rest of the season we brushed the opposition aside, even thrashing the Aldenham Under 14s where unforgettably I took nine wickets, but we never felt the excitement, or the pressure, of being unbeaten. Towards the end of term, Sid asked us for our signatures and then explained that our parents had agreed to a small sum being added to the bill for a present. On the final day he gathered us together in his study with EWE. Jules did the honours:

"Sir, we're all very sorry about the Grimwade game, but we'd still like you to accept this small gift as a token of our thanks for all you've done for us and for this great season." He handed over a blue box which EWE revealed to contain a silver ash tray inscribed "EWE Summer 1958 from …" and there were all our signatures. The poor man was overcome and I can't remember what he said as I, too, was trying to hold the tears back.

Later that day, my parents and I went to say goodbye. "I'll always remember you, Chippo. Good luck at Felsted," he said, and he handed me a little book. It was Bernard Darwin's 'W.G. Grace' inside which he had written in his immaculate script: "N.J. Chapman – In memory of a happy and successful season Heath Mount 1958 – With every good wish from EWE."

I've still got it.

If only he could have written 'unbeaten.'

*

Amazingly, just seven years later, I was helping to run a prep school lst XI. Summer Fields in Oxford were short of a gap student and offered me the job to do a bit of teaching and help with the sport. As a bit of a cricketer I was asked to assist with the top team . The master i/c, Chris Snell, a good cricketer but a better coach, was about six years older than me and was my mentor at the school. We got on fabulously together and the thought of helping him was very appealing.

The boys liked having two young members of staff taking them as our levels of enthusiasm almost matched theirs. Cricket was a religion, as befits a school that over the years has produced a fair selection of major and minor county players, the most distinguished being Gubby Allen. And amongst this year's crop was one destined to captain Sussex and manage two England tours. I was warned this boy was special but I had no idea just how good until I saw him in the nets on the first day of term. He bowled mean seamers at a brisk pace better than most, but as a batsman he had it all – attack or defence, forward or back, every shot in the book and it was a near impossibility to get him out. Johnny Barclay lived and breathed cricket all day long. Whenever you passed his classroom there would be a game going on using his mini bat and a soft ball. And the chances were that Johnny would be batting as he was arguably better indoors than out.

His reputation inevitably preceded him and us around the fixture circuit, where the umpiring could at times be best described as 'interesting'. The match at St Piran's always came early on in the term as they were not among the strongest of opponents, but they did possess a formidable weapon in the person of Colonel Tubner-Jones, an experienced but ageing master-in-charge. We lost the toss and the inevitable insertion followed. Our theory though was it was better to bat first: score the runs quickly, and give yourselves time to bowl the opposition out – the 'proper' way to play cricket! Anyway we invariably chose to bat first and most opponents would put us in, so we got used to it.

Johnny opened the batting and soon looked as comfortable as ever, stroking two cover drives for four in the first over. The Colonel struggled up from square leg to oversee the second over, which, unusually at this early stage, was to be bowled by a leg-spinner. A single off his first ball brought Johnny down to face which he did with his usual serenity as he played three impeccable forward defensives. The fifth ball, though, was quicker and shorter. Johnny went back, tried to turn it to leg but missed and was struck on the pad.

"Howzzat," yelled the bowler. The Colonel's finger shot triumphantly into the air with a confirmatory "Out ... OUT!"

Beaming from ear to ear, he then tottered towards Chris at square leg.

"Sorry about that, Snell. Unplayable ball ... unplayable. Pitched two inches outside leg and would have hit middle and off. Poor lad. Such a good bat."

Now Chris is a very gentle man, kindness personified, never one to make a scene, but even his sang-froid was stretched on this occasion.

"I beg your pardon, Colonel, but did you say the ball pitched two inches outside the leg stump?"

"What?... What? ... No ... no ... no. Ball pitched on the leg stump, turned two inches and would have hit middle and off. Unplayable."

It didn't make any difference. We won easily enough but the enduring memory of the incident was Johnny's reaction. Initially distraught on returning to the pavilion, he quickly recovered his composure and was soon blaming himself for foolishly allowing the ball to hit his pads. Inside it must have hurt badly to have been treated so unfairly, but he never let it show and this philosophical attitude always stayed with him. A wonderful character, even at an early age.

*

Anticipation was high, the excitement great. It was the day of the Horris Hill match and the nerves were beginning to jangle early on in the morning. Break time saw us all out on the square rehearsing fielding positions for each bowler and the final team talk.

This was some twenty years later and now I was running the 2nd XI which enabled me to still play the occasional game of club cricket. The 2nds are always great fun – not too serious, the boys are good enough to know what they're doing and the result is not the be all and end all of the day. But we still liked to win! Especially against Horris Hill.

The Horris 2nd XI is run by a lovely man called David Winther, a real gentleman, an expert coach and without ever showing any emotion totally dedicated to his team and school. He is equally gracious in victory or defeat, but he too likes to win. Especially against Summer Fields.

It is always a huge advantage to play at home as neither school relishes the Oxford/Newbury journey. As ever they arrived late so the game didn't get going until 2.45pm, when upon losing the toss we were invited to bat first. The Horris boys busy themselves with some catching practice and two particularly large specimens bowl at each other. Rather fast and furiously for our lads' liking. David and I wander out to umpire.

"Good luck!" he says.

"Oh," I reply. "Are we going to need it?"

David chuckles. "No, no ... certainly not. I just hope we get as good a game as usual." And with that he departs for the far end tossing the new ball in his hands to officiate for the opening over.

Cricket at Summer Fields in the 1980s

Five overs later Summer Fields manage to score their first run. A bye. Trying desperately hard to remain silent and show the impartiality of an umpire, I am actually rapidly going apoplectic. Both openers have clearly listened to my overtures not to take any risks early on, get a good sight of the bowling and wait for the bad ball. The trouble is there are not many bad balls and both batsmen have retreated into their turtle-like shells, offering not a semblance of an attacking stroke. Luckily this torpor ends two overs later when Oliver Brett manages to pop a soft catch up to gully and our star attacking batsman can enter the affray. One ball later he leaves it, having played the most glorious cover drive only to see his off stump removed. One run, two wickets, eight overs. Panic in the pavilion where torpor is clearly deemed a better bet than aggression.

About an hour later, a streaky inside edge beats stumps, wicket-keeper and long leg, just, to register our first boundary and enables us to reach the dizzy landmark of double figures. 12 for six and the embarrassment of my inept coaching is being exacerbated by the inordinate time each boy remains at the crease before capitulating for a duck. 12 for six soon becomes 12 for seven as both batsmen fail in their negotiations over a run and arrive together at the bowler's end while the wicket-keeper calmly removes the bails at the other. My withering look clearly puts the fear of God into them both as they then exit together. David Winther, in the meantime, is calmness personified at square leg ... but, I strongly suspect, with a hint of a smile on his lips.

It is at this point I come to my senses and realise I can, with total impartiality of course, assist my team. James Maby, having just got that streaky four, is our highest scorer and must remain.

"James," I call, "you're the one not out," and turn to stride off to square leg for the new over. On turning to face the next farcical episode, I am mortified to discover that James Maby is nowhere to be seen and that James Polk has returned to continue his innings.

It was though, of course, a touch of genius. James Polk, never a rapid scorer, gets eight in that very next over! A four through the slips to the untenanted third man boundary with a very respectable angled forward defence – a stroke we had spent hours honing together in the nets; a well run two to long leg, who fumbles it – most un-Horris Hill like; and a two off the last ball – a quick single to mid on very sensibly to retain the strike, only to be overcome with the excitement of an overthrow. Suddenly we had reached the verdant pastures of 20.

It was a false dawn. Numbers 9 and 10 were in the team for their fielding and social skills, not their batting and number 11, no batsman, no social skills but a very fast bowler, stayed long enough to get a leg-bye but no more. James sadly didn't receive another ball. 21 all out. 4.07pm. Total humiliation.

In between the innings the Horris boys badger David to arrange a beer match after the inevitable crushing victory. Our boys are forlorn and silent, waiting for some inspiration from the master i/c, who at this moment of crisis is lost for words. I am woken from my stupor by our sensible captain:

"Well, Sir, what do you think we should do?"

The usual platitudes – runs on the board, never over till the end, etc. – are useless. I say the first thing that comes into my head:

"Believe. Just believe."

And with that, eleven bemused Summerfieldians take the field.

The Horris innings is opened by the tall, formidable-looking Douglas-Pennant, whom our boys well remember striking five sixes in an unbeaten 60-odd to win the Under 11 match the year before. At least he wont get 60-odd this year. In fact, remarkably, he doesn't get any at all. To the first ball, well wide of the off stump, he plays a grandiose and full-blooded off drive with his head in the air ready to watch it sail over the extra cover boundary. He does connect, but only with a thick outside edge. The ball does sail, but in a huge arc straight to our third man who to the joy of the whole team, and the relief of the master i/c, manages to cling on to it. 0 for one. Number 3 is equally tall and formidable-looking but possesses no reputation as yet. He clearly is a very sensible bat as he lets his first three balls go, plays an immaculate forward defence to his fourth, and then unleashes a tremendous straight drive to the final ball of the over. Our opening bowler simply can't get out of the way as the ball whacks him on the foot and ricochets straight on to the stumps at the bowler's end. Joyfully, or sadly, depending on your allegiance, the no. 2 bat has been so well trained at Horris Hill that he is backing up and so is unluckily dismissed without facing a ball. 0 for two and I try hard to disguise the spring in my step on coming in from square leg.

No. 4 is the Horris captain so is bound to be a star performer. He is clearly intent on restoring sanity to this mildly inconvenient situation and plays a very sensible over, leaving four balls well alone and defending the other two with expert precision. Tall and formidable-looking no. 3 in the meantime has obviously been upset by the incident at the end of the first over. He charges down the wicket to his very next ball and is clean bowled. 0 for three. Diminutive no. 5 is hit on the pad first ball. Embarrassingly the whole Summer Fields team yell an appeal and I glare at the fielder standing beside me who grins back and says:

"But he's out, Sir!" And I turn to see David's finger up. 0 for four!!

Excitement amongst the fielders is now at fever pitch. Somehow they have got to be calmed down, after all we're still defending a mere 21. Fortunately the Horris Hill captain does it for us. He marches down the wicket to the new man and gives him a long and serious lecture. Instructions, I suspect, are followed to the letter as neither batsman offers anything that could resemble a risk. The hat trick ball is a wide, so a spell of sorts is broken. A bye follows, then a single (which really should have been two as long leg fumbled), and a streaky snick for four between the wicket-keeper and slip. 7 for four but all this takes about seven or eight overs and the tension is mounting inexorably.

Before I realise it, we have been out in the field for over an hour. The score has crept up ever so slowly as have the wickets. But the captain heroically remains, determined to guide his side to victory. Like all, well, most, Horris Hill boys he is frightfully polite and very sociable. We meet as I approach the stumps to officiate at the bowler's end:

"It's a very good game, isn't it, Sir!"

"Yes," I reply, "it's very exciting, and if I may say so, you yourself are batting extremely well."

15

"Oh, thank you very much, Sir." And smiling contentedly to himself, he neglects to respond in time to his partner's call for a single and fails to make his ground by a good yard or so. 15 for seven.

The next little boy is a bundle of nerves. Bootlace undone, pad flapping with a buckle loose, shirt hanging out. Poor David is totally embarrassed and strides in from square leg to rectify matters. As he returns he suddenly remembers, and asks:

"McQuorkadale, you have got a box on, haven't you?"

The poor child turns puce.

"Oh. N ... n ... no, Sir."

"Well. I think you had better go and put one on."

The fielders titter. The daisies flutter. Some pigeons coo. And the world waits as McQuorkadale slinks back to the pavilion, equips himself with the protective item and eventually returns to the fray. Robbie Henchman, our sensible captain at silly mid off, smiles kindly at him and McQuorkadale obliges by pushing a dolly catch straight to him. 15 for eight.

By now the tension is unbearable. Nerves have rendered useless any ability the remaining batsmen may have, but equally they have started to affect the bowlers for whom an unthinkable victory has now become a real possibility. Straight balls, and there are not many, are stopped. All others are missed. A no-ball makes it 16, two byes should have made it 18 but the receiver is woefully adrift at the bowler's end – one run short. The next ball is hit surprisingly firmly straight to square leg, who fumbles it. The batsmen open negotiations:

"Yes!" shouts the non-striker and hurtles up the wicket.

"No!" bellows the other and remains firmly rooted in his crease.

"Come on!" retorts the first as he approaches his partner.

"No! He's got the ball," shouts the latter, as square leg retrieves the elusive object and hurls it at the wicket-keeper, who breaks the stumps and yells howzzat.

"Not Out!" I shriek from square leg, imploring that moronic idiot to grasp the indisputable fact that not one, but both batsmen were in, at the same end, his end.

Bemused by the situation the wicket-keeper drops the ball, regathers it and wildly flings it at the bowler. In the meantime, the batsmen, realizing this was not a good moment to be socialising both set off at high speed to the other end. Sadly, all was not well with the fielding team as the ball was not heading straight to the bowler, but somewhat to his east, more in the direction of mid off who transfixed by the chaos unfolding before him, was not watching the ball at all. Luckily mid on was an intelligent Eton Scholar, selected for his fielding, social skills and moments like this, and he sprinted from his western viewpoint and dived to stop the errant ball going for what could have been a disastrous four overthrows. The batsmen by now had both reached the bowler's end, gaped horrifically at each other, set off on a return journey, stopped and then, nobly, decided to go their separate ways. Mid off, having come to, picks up the loose ball and unerringly throws down the stumps at the bowler's end, something that in weeks of fielding practices he had never once done before. The whole team throw arms to the heavens and yell an appeal. David, the epitome of sense and decorum, calmly pronounces not out as even I from the other end can see that the batsman had taken up residence a good second or so earlier. With a broad grin David approaches me to discuss matters:

"I'm not sure," he says, "but did they get a run?"

I look at the two batsmen and can't for the life of me remember who had been facing. Eton Scholar, though, has no doubts.

"They've changed ends," he says. And indeed they had. 18 for eight.

One ball remains in the over. It is not a good one, arriving as it does as a juicy full-toss just outside the leg stump. The hero of the previous ball as, judging from the cheers from his team mates in the pavilion, that is how they now regard him for effecting the last run, clearly has ambitions to finish this nonsense off with one final, all conquering blow. He winds himself up, and with a great circular motion, flings his all at the ball. Marvellously, he misses completely, falls over and is comfortably stumped, much to the delight of our wicket-keeper relieved to have so quickly made amends for his recent indiscretion. 18 for nine.

I move into position at the bowler's end, elated at a prospect of an astonishing victory but dreading having to give an LBW as the dénouement.

One run comes early in the over and the groans from the pavilion suggest that the Horris no. 11 is probably not the greatest proponent of the art of batsmanship. Their fears are well grounded but the immensity of the moment is probably too much anyway. The delivery is ordinary, but straight, far too much for the poor lad and he is clean bowled. The Summerfieldians lose all sense of decorum and prance around with joy unbounded. I can't believe it. David comes up, hand outstretched:

17

"Well done," he says, "what a wonderful game!"

It was. It was simply the best prep school game I was ever involved in. Quite unforgettable. Lovely to have won, but in the end it mattered not who won or lost.

*

Many years later as a Headmaster I was lucky enough to have the chance to run two schools steeped in the cricketing tradition. Firstly at Lockers Park, who produced the Nawab of Pataudi, and then, ironically, at Horris Hill where famously Douglas Jardine first played against Gubby Allen. As a Head you have to be dispassionate – show you care, support regularly and loyally, but resist the temptation to interfere. Your most important role is to ensure you have the right master-in-charge, someone obviously who can coach, but who will also highlight enjoyment and participation rather than a simple need to grind out results. Of course you bask in the glory of winning teams but you also have to face the flak if things don't go quite so well. Perhaps the hardest role is controlling parental expectations which have changed for the worse over the years. In the early years simply to see Bertie playing in the Under 11Bs was a thrill for Mum and Dad who would support son and team enthusiastically. Later it was still a thrill, but interest revolved more around "why isn't he in the As?" or "why is he only batting at 5, he's far better than Jones?". Such niceties can tax even the calmest of schoolmasters, so increasingly it becomes the privilege of the Head to cope with such parental frustration.

It was the first match of term and the 1st XI had been published on the Friday evening. Fourteen boys had recently returned from a very enjoyable but, from a cricketing point of view, not particularly successful tour of The Cape. This was no surprise as in South Africa the season was just ending and our lads inevitably struggled despite much hard work in the indoor nets. The benefit, though, was surely to come now. Team selection was not straightforward as anyone with a modest mathematical and cricketing background could calculate that three tourists would miss out.

The red light on the answerphone was flashing persistently. Pressing the replay button revealed a curt, unmistakeable message: "Pennington here. I wish to speak with the Head urgently." Oh. Nice one, I thought. Just what we want on a Friday evening.

Experience tells you to play for time. Take some sting out of the venom. Do a little homework first. Um ... John Pennington, nice enough chap, friendly, supportive parent, had transferred young Guy to us aged 10. Boy quite clever, leaving this term, should sail through his exams, keen cricketer, been on SA tour ... but a quick glance at the list of tomorrow's XI reveals no Pennington. Ah! Let's first have a word with the master i/c.

"Ben ... Nigel here ... sorry to trouble you, but father Pennington wishes to speak to me ... any reason Guy not in the lst tomorrow?"

"No, not really. It's just that his bowling isn't quite good enough and Tom Franks looked better in practice this afternoon. Could have been the other way round but my gut reaction was to go with Tom."

"Fine. Any reaction from Guy when you told them the team?"

"He was understandably disappointed, but I explained this was for the first match, we'd review it all next week, and at least in the 2nd XI he'd open the bowling and would have the chance to prove me wrong."

So! I could guess what was coming. Fortified by a glass of wine, I dialled the Pennington's number.

"Hullo, John. Nigel Chapman here from Horris. You asked me to ring."

"Yes. Guy has phoned, utterly distraught. He tells me he's not in the lst XI tomorrow. I'll have you know we spent a lot of money on that South African Tour and it was not for him to be in the 2nds. I simply will not accept it. Marjorie and I are coming to watch the match tomorrow and you will kindly ensure Guy is playing." And with that the phone was firmly put down!

Joy of joys! And we play cricket for fun!

Of course, there was no decision to be made on what happened, it was just the handling of the parents and taking the inevitable vitriol on the chin. Poor Guy was so embarrassed and it was very obvious he was not the distraught one. Three matches into the term he won his place in the team on merit, but the scowl remained on his Dad's face for some time.

The Elysian Fields of prep school cricket are no longer quite so idyllic.

2. HOME

The Chapmans come from Standon in Hertfordshire, where they ran a flourishing building firm. My father, Leslie, being the youngest of three boys, was never going to have the opportunity of running the company but clearly had building in the blood. He married at the age of 24 into another building family, the Cowlins, of Harlow in Essex and fairly quickly became the proprietor of James Cowlin & Sons. The reason for this was that the owner, Alexander Cowlin, died quite young and had four daughters, but it was only the second, Mary, who had the sense to marry a builder. They married in 1928, built their own house in Standon and my father had to commute to Harlow when he took over Cowlins in the mid-thirties. I was born in 1945 and almost immediately afterwards, my parents moved permanently to live beside the firm's premises in Old Harlow which is where I grew up.

My father was a very quiet, home-loving man to the extent I hardly knew his family. Indeed I met his second brother only once ... at my father's funeral. My mother was much more gregarious and we knew her side far better, often staying and having holidays with the various aunts and cousins. My mother had had a difficult time with her child-bearing, one a boy was still born and a second a girl lived only a few days, before my older brother, Charles, was born in 1937. The war then intervened and as a result with eight years' difference I hardly knew him, grew up almost as an only child and inevitably, in the light of what had happened to her, was a bit precious to my mother.

She was keen and capable at sports in her own right but what talent I inherited undoubtedly came from my father. He was so modest and unassuming that he never spoke about what he had done and I only unearthed it by rootling one day in the attic through old press cuttings, photographs and magazines that my mother had stashed away. He'd been at Newport Grammar School and had got into both the cricket and football lst XIs as a fifteen year old playing and competing with young men three years his senior. The strain on his growth, however, became so much that the medics forbade him to play at all the following year as they felt his heart wouldn't cope with the demands that were being placed on it. But he still became a star, captaining both teams in his final year. He went on to play football for Bishop's Stortford for some 15 years and his greatest moment was when he led them to victory in the Herts Senior Cup in 1933, the first time the club had won it. Cricket was his favourite game but it had to take a back seat as he was in demand to play tennis for Hertfordshire which he kept up until the late 1930s.

Interestingly, especially in the light of what follows in Chapter 6, the majority of the cricket he did play as a young man was of the Old Boy variety, with the Old Newportonian C.C., a club he founded and ran for some ten years before it folded due to lack of support midway through the 1930s. His own cricket only became significant again after the move to Harlow when he became the life-blood of Harlow C.C. who played on the Marigolds ground, which was within walking distance of our home. Over the remaining 29 years of his life he became captain, team manager, chairman and president, for much of the time combining three of the roles at the same time. And it was here that my innate love of the game was nurtured and developed.

Saturday afternoons became a special time. Already changed into his whites, he'd pick up his leather bag, tell me to get my bat, take hold of my hand and we'd walk up to the ground together. There we'd often be before the others so he'd bowl a bit to me before sending me off to the scoreboard which I would contentedly work for the afternoon. Then after the game all the kids would be playing cricket haphazardly together and he and other Dads would come over and organize it better, making sure we were holding the bats right, helping us learn to bowl overarm or having a catching competition. It was bliss, because, as we know, in those days, the sun always shone. Afterwards he'd have a beer, always half a pint of shandy and he'd buy me a ginger beer. Occasionally he'd have a second, rarely, if ever, a third. And then it would be time to go home and contentedly I'd take his hand and we'd wander back together with me longing for the next game to come round as fast as possible.

Quite often it would be the next day. Sunday mornings were always spent at the ground, rolling the square, cutting the grass and generally maintaining the facilities. It was amazing how many of the members would turn out to help. In fact the support was so good that one year early in the 1950s a whole new pavilion was designed and built without any outside assistance. There was a great family atmosphere about the club and it was fun being part of it. My Dad didn't often play on the Sunday as with just one eleven being put out there was a surplus of players available and instead he enjoyed a tennis party at home on the grass court he had spent many hours perfecting. But there was always one Sunday a year he'd be involved and that was the annual trip to play at Clacton-on-Sea. It was the great event on the club's calendar and a coach

'The Pavilion', Marigolds Cricket Ground, Old Harlow
(Harlow Cricket Club ground since the 1890's)

would be hired to take team, families, and supporters for a full day out. In those austere years after the War it was a great treat and everybody looked forward to it.

Sadly, I can hardly recall seeing him bat for any length of time. As captain, he insisted on going in at no. 11, explaining when I asked that all the others had come to have a bat or a bowl and he got his fun out of being the captain. There was just the one occasion when I was about 12 and we batted together for over an hour to save a game that was being hopelessly lost. He kept on telling me to keep the bowling as I was much better and younger than him, but in truth he wasn't in any difficulty at all and far less likely to get out. It was great walking back to the pavilion with him with everyone clapping and he was obviously quite proud, but said nothing bar a 'jolly well done.' But that was more than enough.

My most memorable moment with him though was on the tennis court. He was clearly an outstanding player and even in his fifties when he wasn't so mobile his positional sense and placement of the ball were still masterful. We were on holiday, which in itself was unusual as Dad didn't do holidays, at Thurlestone in Devon. The tennis club there ran a weekly mens doubles competition and my mother for a joke entered Dad and myself. I was 16 at the time and a competent player but no more. We were drawn against a local pair who if they played were always seeded first as they frequently turned out for Devon, and apparently they wanted to play in order to warm up for County Week. Clearly an old man and a young boy would be no problem in round one but they made the error of playing at the old man. Dad had them sorted, told me just to get the ball back and in next to no time we were 3-1 up, 4-2, 5-5 and by now there was quite a crowd hoping to witness a major upset. We kept it up until 7-7 but they had by then cottoned on and started to play on me. They broke my serve and ran out winners 9-7. For half an hour he'd been back in his prime and it had been magic.

The frustrating thing was that I never really got to know him. He was devoted to his work, disappearing early in the morning, coming back for a brief lunch and then staying in his office until late. He said the only time he could get any proper work done was after 5pm when he didn't get disturbed. If I wanted to see him I'd have to go down there and I'm sure that irritated him but he'd never say. He tried hard to get me interested in the firm and during several holidays from school I helped out with some of his paperwork, but it wasn't for me. My brother was training to take over and I knew from an early age I wanted to teach.

My father died, aged just 70, in 1974 after contracting Hodgkin's disease for which in those days there was no cure, and I was distraught. But he'd given me my love of sport and of cricket in particular. He let slip to a friend, never to me, how much pleasure my cricketing successes had given him and it was some solace to be told that. True to his character, he wanted no fuss, no gravestone, just his ashes scattered over the ground he'd come to love so much, the Marigolds Cricket Ground in Old Harlow. I did manage to have some appropriate words written into the Book of Remembrance at the crematorium:

> For when the one Great Scorer comes
> To write against your name
> It matters not who won or lost
> But how you played the game.

My mother lived on to just see in the new century, bravely living and coping by herself for 25 years and I tried to see as much of her as I could but it was never enough. Family ties became increasingly tenuous with my teaching commitments and life being based in Oxford.

*

I was brought up therefore to feel very much part of Harlow C.C. Nowadays clubs have junior sections that are highly organised and very well run by members who have become qualified coaches and who oversee regular fixture lists for each age group. With the difficulty of providing adequate cricket in state schools, clubs are fulfilling a vital function not just in self-preservation but especially in securing the life-blood for the game itself. And a magnificent job they are doing too. In my youth, cricket was still flourishing in all schools. I was lucky to be educated privately but the majority of the youngsters that turned up at Harlow were at state schools where the cricket was an integral part of their summer terms and very good they were too. The club role was different then. It was the Dads' domain but a child's presence was never ignored and once you were old enough, and presumably capable enough, they would try and get you into the 2nd XI. But it was unlikely to happen unless your Dad was involved. Before you reached those dizzy heights you could show your enthusiasm in the scorebox where the eldest would be in charge and two or three others would run around moving the rollers and hanging up the numbers. It was the greatest fun and in doing this you got to know the players so well.

The anticipation and excitement was palpable when Jack Nichols came in at no. 5! He was a real hitter and you'd so hope he would be your side of the board as you just knew you'd be very busy. But if not Jack, then the odds were you'd get Alf Mealing at 6. And he dealt in sixes! Huge ones, straight over the bowlers head into the smart garden of Marigolds House behind the fence. What a pair those two made. They really were our heroes. But mind you, some weeks they might not get in. The openers Frank Debenham and Bill Austin were so difficult to get out that they frequently put on 100 for the first wicket and I lost count of the times I had to manoeuvre a 1 in its long-handled guider to the top of the scoreboard to indicate a century to one or the other. And even if they did get out there was Freddie Brooks at no. 3. He was a bank teller and clearly only dealt in high scores. He was followed by Lou Freeman, a stylish fast scorer, not a crude striker of the ball like Jack, but a stroker and placer of the ball. Then at no. 7 was Freddie Silcock, just the man for a crisis. He was so quiet and calm with a slow, languid, slightly bow-legged gait, nothing ever bothered him. He batted left-handed and bowled left-arm seamers and was probably the best of the lot. Then there was Michael Davey, a teenager when he was first drafted in. Tall, thin, angular and red-headed he bowled off-spin so balanced the side perfectly especially as he could bat a bit too. At 9 there was the terrifying Frank Carruthers, a huge hulk of muscle who opened the bowling with Jack, but always downhill at lightning speed. The no. 10 would generally be someone different each week, invariably a bowler as Dad could ensure he got into the game, but it would be the place to give someone from the 2nd XI who had been doing well. And of course Dad himself would be at no. 11, and it was no wonder I rarely saw him bat!

As a six/seven year old these were my heroes! And a mighty team they were. Alf was my favourite because of the sixes, but he was the wicket-keeper too so was in the thick of the action all the time and he was especially friendly. He always had a smile on his face and was invariably cracking jokes. Freddie Silcock was the kindest as he often helped coach me. I think he took a special interest in me as I batted left-handed like him. But they were all so nice, which I grew to realise when a bit older as I was allowed to travel to away games as the scorer. We'd meet up at Deard's garage on the A11 in the middle of the town where two taxis would be ready to take us wherever. They'd all chat away during the journey and they'd certainly not leave me out especially when it got onto football as they knew I supported Arsenal. Then at the match when we were batting, one or more of them would come along to see if I was all right, had the names right and was keeping up. When we were fielding I just had to cope but they knew I could otherwise I would not have been allowed to do it.

Then one day, late morning, just before going to meet up at Deard's, Dad said 'I think you'd better take your kit, as I'm not sure Lou is going to make it today.' I must have been 12 that year, and the thought of playing with these people I'd looked up to for so long was terrifying! I think Dad knew all along as there was no sign of Lou. I didn't have to bat, but it was thrilling enough just to field. It was a clever way of getting me involved and showed the advantage of having your Dad as captain and team manager!

*

From then on I started to play for Harlow as often as possible. It was never regularly as I was away at boarding school so it was just during the holidays. Inevitably the first year or two were in the 2nd XI but by the age of 15 it was invariably in the first team. It was always cleverly managed that no-one would be dropped to make way for me, I would simply be the person in July, August and early September to replace the one off injured or away on holiday. It worked perfectly and slowly I made my way up the batting order. The team of course was gradually changing. Lew Whitby, Peter Prodger and Bob Waller, became three new stalwarts of the club but Alf, Jack, Michael and Freddie Silcock remained. Dad stopped playing but stayed at the hub of affairs as team manager while

Lew became the captain. It was a seamless transformation and the club continued in its same old friendly way.

No Leagues were needed as the games were competitive enough and in particular the captaincy positive enough, on both sides, to ensure decent contests. And helmets weren't given a thought, although the pitches could best be described as interesting and the ball was liable to fly around. Cricket was just different in those days and there was no question it was hugely enjoyable. None of us would pretend that Harlow was in the upper echelons of club cricket in Essex, but the standard was not bad. The critics of the next, and subsequent generations, would say it was not competitive enough, not least because the result didn't matter. Hence the advent of Leagues but it depends on what you want. Nowadays most club cricketers relish the cut and thrust of competition, where the result, or at least the points gained (or denied) are the be all and end all of the day's entertainment. In the fifties and sixties I suggest the greater pleasure came from the game itself, whereby you were happier to have lost a game narrowly in the final overs than to win by some large margin in a non-event. A draw was a genuine result and often the most exciting one.

I was roundly criticised, and correctly, when I started playing some games for Essex 2nd XI by Frank Rist, the County Coach at the time, as he said that my cricket would not improve if I continued to play at Harlow. He said I ought to come and play for Walthamstow where the cricket was of a much higher standard. I have no doubt he was right. But his argument would have made much more sense had he suggested a club he wasn't so closely involved with himself, so there were doubts at the back of my mind as to his motives. Added to which was the loyalty I owed my father and his club. It was difficult and I suspect I took the easy way out by staying put. In my misguided arrogance I felt as long as I was playing decent cricket I would be fine, but I really only learnt how wrong I was when I joined North Oxford as late as 1971. But that was still way in the future, and by then my circumstances were totally different. I learnt to love the game at Harlow, thanks largely to my Dad and the friendly characters around him. And, above all, I learnt to play the game for fun, a philosophy that was to be developed even further in my years at Felsted.

*

My connection with Felsted started some time before I arrived as a pupil in 1958. My mother was keen to encourage my cricket in any way she could and after I had got into the Heath Mount lst XI aged nine, approached the Felsted cricket professional, 'Mac' Gough, to ask if he would be prepared to coach me during the Easter holidays. 'Mac' agreed but only on condition that I was coming on to his school in due course, which as my brother was already there was certainly being planned. So each April from 1956 my mother would drive the 18 miles to and from Felsted each day for a week so I could have a two hour session with 'Mac'. There would often be two or three others there, notably Roger Luckin who was soon to play for Essex, but we'd always be guaranteed half an hour's individual batting attention. 'Mac' was a stickler for detail and accuracy. He'd chuck balls down endlessly at you to hone a particular shot to perfection and even then he'd probably not be satisfied. He was a marvellous coach and so patient. I gathered later on he was not the easiest man to get on with but to me in those days he was God and my cricket owed a very great deal to him. It was interesting how Roger, even when he was playing with Essex, would go back to 'Mac' to iron out any problem. He retired in 1960 but kept the Easter session going for two more years until he became ill. He died in 1963 and I missed his warmth and friendliness and above all his ability to spot what you were doing wrong and put it right. At least he was still around to see his protégé get into the Felsted 1st XI, and very chuffed he was too. But no pat on the back or anything like that. Just a 'mind you keep that bat straight, young man.'

3. HALCYON DAYS

It was Saturday, 13th May, 1961. I was going to play in the lst XI for the very first time. And I was nervous. Still aged 15 I was the youngest in the team. There were seven 17/18 year olds, mostly experienced lst team players, and four newcomers all about 16 who doubtless were just as apprehensive. Felsted had a good reputation as a cricket school, but in recent years had not done especially well. This year looked promising, not least because the School had appointed the old Essex all-rounder, Ray Smith, to be the coach and assist John Cockett, the experienced master i/c who himself had played to a high level with a Blue at Cambridge and Minor Counties caps to his name.

The first match of the season was designed to be a sort of warm-up game, against a local club side, Hoffman's Athletic, who could be relied upon to play the game in a friendly way and were competent but not too good. In fact their victory the previous season had been their first for a number of years. They won the toss and as usual, probably by arrangement, put us in.

Things did not go well and we lost several wickets quite quickly, to the extent that with the score at 90 for six. I was called upon to bat somewhat earlier than anticipated. In retrospect it was probably a good thing from a personal point of view, as I didn't have time to think about it. At the crease was one of the other new youngsters, Roger Nokes, a really promising batsman, and he had already contributed nobly to a sixth wicket partnership of 25. Batting very carefully we took the score to 109 for six at lunch. Mr Cockett was pleased with us and told us to continue in the same vein for twenty minutes or so after lunch and then try to speed things up. As it turned out, the runs seemed to flow easily, perhaps the wicket had eased, and before long Roger had sailed past his 50 and was heading towards three figures. It was the innocence of youth. We had no inhibitions and just went for our shots. Soon 200 was up and in all we put on 114 before, sadly, Roger was caught on 91. I was on 40 and was allowed to get my 50 before the declaration on 228 for seven.

Any joy or self-satisfaction was quickly squashed as I was ticked off for not helping Roger more to get his ton. Apparently I had kept him off strike too long towards the end of his innings and should have spotted he was getting increasingly nervous. I should have been looking more for singles. I think it went over my head at the time, but two seasons later when he still hadn't scored a century those words did come back to haunt me. In fact he never played so well again. My fault?

Hoffman's found our opening attack – speed at one end and swing at the other – too hot to handle, and although they only lost two wickets early on, they were soon well behind the rate required. At this point the captain, Robert Hunter, handed me the ball and said "Come on, tempt them with some leg-spin."

It helped that in my first over, their captain danced down the wicket, tried to turn a fairly innocuous ball to leg, and got an outside edge which lobbed straight back to me. Thereafter the batsmen, one after another, just seemed to be mesmerized. They clearly hadn't come across leg-spin bowling before. Luckily I could bowl a googly, a pretty obvious one admittedly, but they couldn't spot it. Two got bowled shouldering arms which only made things worse for them. I finished with the figures of 13 overs, 8 maidens, 11 runs, 5 wickets. I couldn't believe it. This 1st XI cricket was a doddle!

Not for long. I was still basking in the kudos of leading the team off to a lot of applause, when Robert took me aside.

Felsted 1st XI, 1961
Ray Smith is back row left, John Cockett back row right,
the author back row fourth from left

"Well done," he said, "that was brilliant. But it was easy. It was easy because nobody, least of all yourself, expected it and the opposition weren't particularly good. You won't be any good until you can score fifties and take five wickets regularly. Get back in those nets and keep practising. But for now, jolly well done."

Wise words and a lovely chap, one of the best captains I played under. And he was right. It was eight matches later before I took five wickets again ... and I didn't get another fifty that year. But he led the side with such skill and modesty that we went from strength to strength winning 12 of the 14 matches, five by over 100 runs, and losing just the once.

*

Twelve months later and the four youngsters were now the core of the team. We were all too young still to be considered for the captaincy, so a senior 2nd XI player was appointed. Richard Oliver had already played hockey for Essex so certainly commanded respect even if he wasn't much of a cricketer. He was a natural, brilliant fielder and could hit a ball hard and far, if not that often, and would need tactical assistance, but we all liked him so it was no problem and it led to a happy and successful season.

Aldenham were among the weaker school opponents, but they didn't like to be beaten and rarely went down without a fight. In those days it was a two day game, an event much anticipated by the visiting side as it meant two full days off school! They won the toss and elected to bat, but took an inordinate time, some 80 overs, to get 201. We batted on into the second morning before declaring after 70 overs with a lead of 51. Aldenham fared better in their second innings, largely thanks to their skipper, Peter Leaver, who scored 87 despite batting with an injured knee. They were finally all out around four o'clock for 258, leaving us 208 to win in less than two hours batting time. Sadly, the rule of twenty overs in the final hour had yet to be introduced.

There was an awkward 15 minutes before tea in which I and my opening partner Doug Smith, who had scored a century in the first innings, were circumspect and we didn't really launch into the bowling until after the interval. Doug was caught and bowled by their off-spinner for 37 when the score was 74. Roger Nokes came in and we were needing about two runs a minute, and despite some agonisingly slow field placing and bowling changes we managed to keep up with the rate largely through a lot of well taken singles. The return of the opening bowlers with thirty minutes left and 50 still required, slowed our scoring and the tension began to rise, not least because each over seemed to take longer and longer to bowl.

The Felsted ground sits conspicuously in front of the rather drab and uninspiring Victorian main building, not an architectural masterpiece by any stretch of the imagination, but a magnificently dramatic setting for a cricket field. And on occasions like this, when the climax to a game becomes interesting, faces start to appear out of the many study and Common Room windows, and clusters of boys collect in groups on the drive surrounding the field as word spreads and supporters emerge from their Houses to see the drama unfold. The atmosphere became increasingly electric and partisan as it was clear to even the most innocent bystander that Aldenham were utilising whatever delaying tactics they could. Their fastest bowler, Mike Nutting, was clearly an expert as he retied his bootlaces, lost his run up, failed to deliver the ball, changed from over to around the wicket, anything to get the clock to reach half past six before the seemingly inevitable Felsted victory.

Roger and I had no option but to fling the bat at everything, and with the field spread far and wide we rode our luck with the ball dropping often in the many open spaces rather than going to hand. To the consternation of the by now large crowd, and not least myself, Roger was caught in the deep for an excellent 45. It was off the fifth ball of Mike Nutting's over, four runs were still needed and there were two minutes left on the clock. Dick Oliver sprinted to the crease and was ready to face before Roger had even left the field of play.

It was at this moment that Ray Smith, umpiring at Nutting's end, came into his own. After all, you don't play 419 games for Essex and not learn a trick or two about the niceties of the game. Above all he was able to keep his head at the critical moment. The bowler thought he had the answer. He deliberately stepped a good foot or so over the crease as he flung the ball wildly down the leg side, inevitably causing Dick to miss. Unquestionably it was a no-ball, arguably it was also a wide. Mike turned and faced the inscrutable Ray Smith, awaiting his call. Ray, falling back on all his 22 years professional expertise, smiled sweetly, and called out loud and clear "OVER."

Mike was dumbfounded. Their umpire, to be fair, totally embarrassed by all the histrionics, marched smartly in from square leg to ensure one more over would be bowled. Off the third ball I hit the winning boundary to finish on 117 not out, my first ever century, but more important than that, we thoroughly deserved to win.

*

The annual fixture against the MCC tended to be a slightly awkward affair. They were understandably always a very strong side, but often an unbalanced one, packed with batting but a bit short of bowlers. This inevitably meant a lot of runs, delicate declarations and the odds favouring the side batting second. John Cockett always played for them which I never thought helped the school much as he obviously knew our strengths and weaknesses which only aided the already powerful opposition. It was nice for him to have a game during term-time and great was the joy for anyone lucky enough to get him out, but I felt we needed his acumen on our side.

The game in 1961 was a fabulous one. The MCC batting first scored 243 for eight, thanks largely to John getting 57 and Tim Higgins, an Old Boy, who played for Cambridgeshire, 78 not out. This was a surprise as Tim, a left-arm spinner of no mean ability was not now known for his batting. Clearly plenty of cheap runs off me that day! We started well and on 169 for four looked well placed for victory, but the rot set in and the last pair came together with 53 still needed. Remarkably these two accepted the challenge and the match was won by the school on the fourth ball of the last over. This was the school's first victory in the fixture for 10 years.

The following year was not so eventful. We declared on 245 for four, which the MCC reached for six with half an hour to spare. John Thicknesse, the Daily Telegraph correspondent, had come both to play and report the fixture. His comment that the track was the fastest in Europe bar Le Mans caused amusement; he certainly liked it, reaching 47 not out in twenty minutes, mostly by putting his foot down the wicket and hitting the ball straight back over the bowler's head.

Doubtless we remembered this the next year. On winning the toss the MCC chose to bat, again on a good wicket. They were soon in trouble, and lost their first five wickets for 47. A partial recovery was followed by a sparkling seventh wicket partnership of 159 in seventy minutes of which John contributed a masterly 68 not out. We boys though felt they had batted on to put the game just beyond our reach, as they finally declared on 282 for six, leaving us to score at over 100 an hour. Doug and I faced an awkward twenty minutes before the tea interval and after a quick team discussion, we determined that the priority was to keep our wickets intact. We felt sure they wanted us to go hell for leather for the runs, and get ourselves out in the process. We weren't going to fall into that trap and were 23 for nought at the break. Thereafter we made a decent fist of the chase without ever looking like reaching the target and the game petered out into a dull draw with us eight wickets down and 50 runs short. There simply hadn't been enough time either for us to get the runs or them to bowl us out ... unless we threw our wickets away, which we weren't prepared to do. A poor game, overshadowed by defensive tactics, but at least we didn't lose.

The next morning I had just come out of the last lesson before break, when I bumped into John.

"Ah, Nigel. I need a quick word."

We went into his classroom, and John shut the door.

"I think you ought to know," he said, "that your conduct of the match yesterday was a disgrace. The MCC simply couldn't understand what you were up to. You and Doug wasted the time before tea just patting the ball back, when you should have got to 50 or 60. With that sort of start you could have won the match. As it was, the game was a write-off."

I couldn't believe what I was hearing.

"Hang on a moment, Sir," I replied. "There are two sides to this. We felt, and we did discuss it together as a team before we went out to bat, that you had batted on far too long and were hoping some of us would throw our wickets away chasing that huge total. We weren't going to fall for that."

"I'm not interested in team discussions," he replied, "you are the captain, and you are responsible. You got it wrong, badly wrong, with the decision to play safe. It's not the way we play cricket here and quite frankly it was embarrassing. I'm not going to say any more about it. Learn from it, and just make sure it never happens again."

And with that, he walked out of the room.

To be fair he never mentioned the matter again.

A few years later, after several pints in The Chequers, I dared to recall the incident with him.

"What you really wanted was to see us lose that game in the final over by five to ten runs," I ventured to suggest.

"What I wanted," he replied, "was for you to be within five to ten runs at the start of the final over. And then, I think you'd agree, even you wouldn't have worried who won."

Of course, as usual, he was right. And that was the way we were taught to play the game.

*

Appropriately, John's ideal scenario unfolded magically in another game right at the end of that same term. Colchester and East Essex were arguably one of the strongest club sides in the county at the time, with several who had played at county or minor county level. They did us the honour of bringing virtually their full 1st team.

The School win the toss and choose to bat first. Despite struggling initially at 16 for three, there is strong support in the middle order to enable us to declare on 241 for eight, leaving our visitors to score at 90 runs an hour to win. Their county players ensure they keep up with the clock but wickets fall at regular intervals to keep both sides interested in forcing a victory. When the seventh wicket falls, 34 runs are needed in 18 minutes. The no. 9 is none other than Ted Phillips who had played cricket for Suffolk, but more famously scored the goals that enabled Alf Ramsey's Ipswich to win the First Division a year earlier. He is a formidable opening bowler but only knows one way to bat. 26 are rapidly scored before his partner is run out, and then in the following over Ted is bowled. We reach the final over of the day with Colchester requiring 8 to win with the last pair at the crease.

A single comes from the first ball, nothing from the second. Two more singles follow off the next two balls. Five to win off two balls. Horror of horrors, the next is a no-ball, off which a single is scampered. The tension is now almost unbearable as a misfield leads to another single. The final ball. Two to win and all four results are still possible. There are four close catchers and the remaining fielders in an outer ring encircling the wicket saving two. The ball is straight, just short of a length. It is prodded to leg, but not fine enough to beat the man behind square. They manage a single but with the ball speedily and safely returned to the keeper, there is no way they can get two, and they don't even attempt it. Match drawn, with the scores level! And who says draws are boring!

This kind of scenario is rare, if not impossible, in schools' cricket today with most matches restricted to a certain number of overs to ensure a result. The problem lies not with the game of cricket itself but in the people who run it, whose defensive attitude puts the priority in the avoidance of defeat. Some would call this a professional approach. Certainly the game is played much harder in schools nowadays, and I have no doubt it is much better technically, but it has lost a lot of the fun.

*

It was the greatest fun in those days and there was no doubt we all thoroughly enjoyed our cricket. We won most matches, lost a few and didn't have that many draws. But looking back it was a very amateur approach and really it was no surprise that Felsted produced so few first-class cricketers before Gordon Barker was appointed coach. This lack of professionalism really came home to me the following season, my fourth in the XI and second as captain. That in itself was an error. I needed to be playing serious club cricket on a regular basis, and it was a wasted term from a cricketing angle.

Mill Hill were one of our regular school opponents, and they were normally a very respectable team, particularly difficult to beat on their own ground in North London. We didn't like their slow, seamer friendly track in the same way they didn't appreciate our flat, true surface conducive to quick scoring. At home we could score plentifully, at Mill Hill you had to grind out a score. Their master-in-charge was Oliver Wait, a huge, fair-haired man with a friendly disposition. He was a fiendishly accurate seamer, who had won two Blues at Cambridge, and played for Surrey. John and he knew each other well from their Cambridge days and got on, which meant the games were always keenly contested but played in the right spirit. Despite this, Oliver's approach to the game was very different. It was decidedly professional.

In 1964 the fixture was played at Felsted, but there had been a fair amount of rain and the start had to be delayed until after lunch. In the previous two years I had scored quite a few runs in the game, a fact that had not gone unnoted by Oliver, and unbeknown to me he had laid plans accordingly.

Felsted won the toss and as usual I opened the batting. Our first 20 came up pretty quickly of which I had scored 16. Their opening bowler, a fairly innocuous medium-pace trundler, seemed to be aiming at my legs which was fine as a couple had already been dispatched to the boundary. And then came another half-volley, just outside the leg-stump, which I whipped off my pads ... only to see it go straight to a leg gully, just slightly backward of square, who caught it. Amidst cries of 'Yes!' the rest of the team surrounded bowler and fielder showing no little excess of joy and delight. In the meantime I slunk off with my tail between my legs.

Some twenty minutes later, after I had got over the disappointment of my cheap demise, John sidled up to me and suggested I asked Mr Wait about the dismissal. Which I did.

"I'm sorry," he said, "but I've seen you bat too much in recent years, so we laid a trap. As we won't have to bowl to you again I can tell you! I don't know whether you realise, but whenever you play to the leg, your weight falls away to the off. This inevitably means that a lot of your leg-side shots go in the air, particularly behind square. Try opening out your stance a little bit, that should help."

The Felsted way won through though. As we've seen, John's mantra was 'attack.' Score fast and get through your overs fast. We declared after 40 overs on 206 for five thanks to a superb century from Richard Dunstan, a lovely chap and excellent batsman, who sadly was to be killed in the 9/11 tragedy in New York. Oliver Wait's expert coaching of his bowlers clearly didn't extend to his batsmen and although it took 55 overs we managed to bowl them out for 173 with just under ten minutes remaining. We simply played the game too quickly for them. Ever the gentleman, Oliver came up afterwards to congratulate me on my 7-49 and our victory. "Well done," he said, "there's not much wrong with the game when it's played the way you lot do."

There was an interesting sequel to Oliver's wise words about my batting two years later when I spent the summer with Essex. Early in April, I and three or four other hangers-on were invited to be with the 1st team when they went to Fenners for an unofficial practice day with Cambridge University. There was no structure to our day beyond sharing 12th man duties. Gordon Barker, though, once he had had his knock, was not going to waste time and grabbed a couple of us to have a net with him. The moment he saw me bat, he said my weight distribution was all wrong. He flung balls at me for some fifteen minutes, got me to open out more, stand up straight and lean my front shoulder into the ball. I learnt more in those fifteen minutes than at any other time with any other coach, and it was a huge sadness that it was the only occasion I was able to have time with him in a net. And even then it had been entirely his idea and of his own volition. His subsequent success with the Felsted teams of the 70s and 80s came as no surprise. He was a natural coach, and one of the very best.

4. LORD'S

It was July 1963 and the letter arrived from the MCC about a fortnight before the end of term:

> Dear Chapman
> I am pleased to inform you that you have been selected to represent The Rest to play Southern Schools at Lord's on the 5th and 6th August. I should be grateful if you could let me know as soon as possible whether you are able to play.
> Yours sincerely,
> J.G. Dunbar (Asst. Secretary Cricket)

It was a stomach-churning moment. I'd never been to the ground, let alone played at anywhere so famous. Obviously I'd seen pictures and watched games on tele, but this was a real thrill, enhanced by the selection also of my friend and opening partner Doug Smith. To have two players selected in the same year was special and both John Cockett and Ray Smith were delighted, but they kept our feet firmly on the ground by emphasizing we now had to perform in order to get into the Schools' XI which would be selected from the 22 in this trial.

It was nerve-wracking as we arrived at The Grace Gates which were promptly opened once we explained our purpose and drove inside. Dad was especially chuffed getting in, and parking behind the Pavilion, free of charge! I made my way to the Pavilion where the doorman explained it would be easier if I went to the other entrance as The Rest were in the Visitors' dressing-room.. It was a curious sensation entering this famous building. The history oozed out of every corner, the huge portraits of the great and the good stared down at you as though questioning your right to enter, and a curious, rubbery smell seemed all pervading. I was directed up two flights of extremely wide stairs to a frosted-glass panelled door which had the reassuring sign of 'Visitors' above it. Tentatively I pushed it opened whilst still lugging my bag, which was getting heavier by the second, and was greeted by a warm, smiling and bespectacled young man.

"Hello," he said, "welcome! I'm David Bailey, the captain, and you must be ..." and he looked down at his list.

"Nigel Chapman," I said to save him any awkwardness, "from Felsted."

"Ah, yes, Nigel. Find yourself a space to get changed ... there's plenty of room ... but there are still four more to arrive."

I couldn't believe the amount of space. The room was enormous, with leather sofas all round the sides of the room and a couple of large tables in the middle. I chose a vacant spot in the right hand corner to put my bag and wandered to the open doors that led to a comparatively small balcony. And ... wow! There was this awe-inspiring ground, the lush green of the grass, immaculately mown in broad strips, contrasting vividly with the white seating spread out all around, way below me. Inevitably the ground was all but empty with just a few people milling around in front of the old Tavern, yet to be demolished. And there was Father Time, on top of the famous scoreboard in the centre of the old Grandstand. It was an amazing vista.

I was brought out of my reverie with a slap on the back. It was Doug. "Hi, old pal, this has come for us." And he thrust a piece of paper at me. It was a telegram from Ray Smith wishing us both the best of luck. Trust him not to forget us on our big day.

Soon introductions were over, David had won the toss and we were batting. How a batting order was worked out I've no idea as inevitably with supposedly the best schoolboy cricketers of the year on show virtually everyone, in fact all bar one, professed to be a batsman and most could bowl. I was down for no. 9, with Doug at 3. In fact it was not an easy wicket to bat on, and the opposition, especially in the person of Andrew Barker, a left-arm spinner, bowled particularly well. We lost wickets regularly, Doug sadly only got one, and soon after lunch at 95 for seven I was required to bat.

You certainly need your wits about you to find your way for the very first time out onto the field of play, and on seeing the wicket fall you have to get a move on. There's the famous story of David Steele going down one flight of stairs too many and finding himself in the Gent's cloakroom. Easily done! Two flights and then through another glass panelled door into the Long Room, which is huge with lots of Members standing around and staring at you as you try to thread your way through to the central doors that lead out to the field of play. All quite terrifying! And then out onto the grass which seems surprisingly soft and spongy and all the way to the wicket, which is a long way as it's right at the very bottom of the square, in front of the Tavern, where what spectators there are have gathered. I assume my parents are among them but I can't see them and anyway I'm far too pre-occupied taking guard to face

Andrew Barker bowling from the Nursery End. It's a huge advantage being a left-hander facing such a bowler. The first ball I receive is all but a half-volley, turning to leg, which I reach out to and place firmly between mid on and mid-wicket and it races away to the very short boundary. Phew! Off the mark! A four and immediately I feel happy and relaxed. Thereafter, the runs flow surprisingly quickly and easily and I'm quite pleased with my 31, the highest score of the innings, before I'm the last man out with the score on 134, clean bowled by Andrew who returns the impressive figures of 7-43.

Fielding in this remarkable arena is another experience, and I am able to appreciate for the first time the extraordinary slope that runs down some eight feet from the Grandstand to the Tavern. You can see it best looking at the Pavilion from the Nursery End. The grass is level with the base of the white railings at the top end, whereas at the bottom it is some four feet below it with a very distinct incline for a ball to climb before claiming a boundary. Clearly I need to bowl my leg-spin from the Nursery End. The outfield, too, is smoother and truer than any ground I'd been on before – no excuse for any poor fielding here!

The Southern Schools find batting no easier and lose wickets regularly. I am on first change but only get the one wicket at an expensive rate of more than four an over. Doug claims one scalp, Graham Roope, and only concedes eleven runs in his eight overs. The damage is done by our skipper who claims 5-40 in thirty overs and at one stage they are 65 for six. But a sparkling partnership between Nick Pretzlik and Andrew Barker doubles the score and they eventually finish on 193, a lead of 59.

In the second innings I'm promoted to no. 4, and score a quick 15 in a partnership of 20 before being bowled. Doug again only manages one, and the team struggle to 146. The Southern Schools knock the runs off without losing a wicket. Sadly, it was an unbalanced match which meant the selectors' choice of the Schools' XI would to some extent have to be based on records throughout the term.

Not long after the game, Mr Dunbar seeks me out to say that sadly I hadn't quite made the team but they'd like me to come back for the following two days for the fixture against the Combined Services and be the official 12th man. I was disappointed to miss out but pleased to have got so close. In fact I had already been asked to play for the Essex Y.A. XI so politely asked not to be 12th man, which he understood. As soon as he went, a wizened old man with a lovely, kind face came up and said how sorry he was I hadn't been selected. Would I like to play for his XI against the English Schools Cricket Association XI here next week. Of course I would and thanked him profusely. He was delighted and hoped it would make up a bit for not getting a Schools' Cap ... try to be here by 10am next Tuesday and go this time to the Home dressing-room. He'd much look forward to seeing me again then.

Well! That was wonderful. But who was he?! I vaguely recognised him but couldn't put a name to him and hadn't dared ask as clearly he was very important and famous. I went back to our dressing-room where David Bailey put me out of my misery and said he was playing too. It was none other than Harry Altham.

I didn't score many runs for him but bowled pretty well to get 3-58 off 25 overs in a close and well contested drawn game. But the remarkable thing was that then he did everything he could to get me into Oxford, writing to dons he knew and getting me interviews at both Trinity and St Edmund Hall. Sadly, my A Levels didn't match his enthusiasm and support so it came to nothing, but he regularly kept in touch until he died two years later in 1965.

*

Three days playing at Lord's were then unexpectedly followed by two more later that month when I was included in the Essex II team to play Middlesex II. Apparently in those days the 2nd XI were allocated one match a season on the hallowed turf and they tried to give each opposition county the opportunity to play there too. In 1963 it was the turn of Essex.

The Essex side was skippered by Arnold Quick who had played a number of times for the county before and after the war. He helped out nowadays by captaining the 2nd XI whenever he was available. It was quite a strong side containing several of the young pros currently on the staff. Middlesex were similar and they were captained by Jack Robertson, a stalwart of the county who had played for England in the late forties and who now ran their 2nd team full-time.

The talk, and concern, in the Essex dressing-room beforehand though was about this young, black fast bowler from Dominica, Pat Lawrence, who had recently joined Middlesex. Apparently, he wasn't very tall but bowled at a ferocious speed and was more than capable of getting the ball up into the ribs.

We won the toss and chose to bat. I was due in at no. 4 so was able to get some sort of preview of what Mr Lawrence had in store for us. He was certainly very quick, but not that accurate so although he got an early wicket caught behind, Essex progressed fairly comfortably onto 61 before I was required. Luckily the wicket had fallen on the last ball of the over so I was able to watch as the non-striker while Pat Lawrence bowled his next over from the Pavilion end. He appeared even quicker out in the middle but Graham Saville was facing and by now seemed to have the hang of him, leaving most well alone and pushing a single wide of mid on from the fifth ball.

If my stomach was churning as Pat Lawrence charged in, it was somewhat worse when the ball thwacked into the keeper's gloves. I simply hadn't seen it at all! It was not a pleasant sensation and I nervously wandered towards Graham to confess the problem.

"Didn't see that at all," I said, "how do you cope?"

"No, it's not easy," he replied, "but you'll get used to it. The problem is he's coming straight out of the brickwork."

I went back to my end and checked and, yes, his bowling hand would be coming straight out of the dark red background of the lower end of the Pavilion. We were on virtually the last wicket at the bottom of the square and there was nothing one could do about that background. Added to that, it was not a very bright day. Great! Probably the fastest bowler I'd ever faced and I can't see the ball! I scratched around for sometime and thanks to Graham taking most of Pat Lawrence we put on 36 before another invisible missile made a complete mess of my stumps. Bowled Lawrence 8 and I made the lengthy way back to the dressing-room conscious I had not made a very good impression. To be fair only Graham (43) and Brian Edmeades (51 not out) got at all set but with a slow outfield and inclement weather, our 149 for six dec. was a better score than it appeared.

This was soon proved to be the case as Middlesex crumbled to Robin Hobbs' leg-spin. Only Clive Radley made an impression with 31 not out and they were all out for 93.

Pat Lawrence was inevitably bowling from the Pavilion end again in the second innings, quickly getting his first scalp caught at the wicket in his first over. I was at the crease soon after, determined this time to be more positive. I got a streaky four past third man and a two wide of long leg but was soon bowled all ends up again. I just didn't see it. It was a curious sensation hanging a straight bat out in front of you hoping to make contact but not having much idea where the ball was.

Luckily others could cope – Tony Steward and Brian Edmeades put on about 70 for the fifth wicket which enabled us to declare on 136 for five, leaving Middlesex 190 to win. They were destroyed in a spectacular opening burst from Denis Sayers who got 4-5 off six overs and with the wicket taking spin Robin Hobbs and Pete Lindsey soon had them 48 for nine. A few speculative blows brought mild respectability but we ran out impressive winners by 116 runs.

It had been a strange experience, my debut in the Essex 2nd XI, playing amidst some remarkably good cricketers and facing a bowler I couldn't see. Pat Lawrence disappeared off the scene almost as quickly as he appeared on it. He played a handful of games for Middlesex the following year, but never mastered enough control to go with his undoubtedly impressive speed, so they released him soon after. At least I didn't have to face him again, but I will never know whether it was his pace or the background that made me look so inept.

*

A year later there was another letter from Mr Dunbar, but this time with a subtle difference. He was inviting me not just to play in the Rest XI but also to captain it. It was a great honour and meant we needed to arrive somewhat earlier to greet the team. I'd been sent a list of those selected with basic details of what they did but with eleven batsmen and seven bowlers it was going to require no little diplomacy to give everyone a fair chance. Luckily the batting order had been laid down but the bowling was thrown awry when John Hutton arrived to announce that he was injured and couldn't bowl. John, the younger son of Sir Leonard, was reputedly very quick and had been ear-marked to open the bowling. The selectors were not best pleased when they heard but got round the problem by swapping John with Pat Neate so you had the geographical anomaly of a Reptonian playing for the Southern Schools and a Pauline for the Rest.

The captain of the Southern Schools was Rupert Daniels, a very friendly and charming Etonian, with whom I got on at once. We quickly discovered that we had something in common. Before Eton he'd been at Summer Fields, the prep school in North Oxford where I was due to go the following term as a Gap student. Over the next few days he was able to fill me in with a lot of background information about the school and the characters who worked there. But more immediately he won the toss and quite rightly chose to bat, which meant my captaincy skills would be immediately put to the test.

On paper the Southern Schools looked to be the stronger side and the way they batted that first innings rather proved the case. Graham Roope, from Bradfield and a Schools' XI cap from the year before, led the way with a speedy 32 but the outstanding knock came from Rupert himself with a superb century in even time. I tried all seven bowlers but none looked especially dangerous and it was all we could do to restrict them to just over three runs an over. When Mike Hooper, from Charterhouse, drove yet another boundary to reach his 50, Rupert declared on 334 for seven. The one really impressive performance in the field came from our wicket-keeper, Roger Tolchard, a Malvernian, who conceded not a single bye.

I was delighted to be opening our innings with Philip Spray, whom I knew well from some close Felsted/Bedford encounters in recent years. Philip was a fine all-rounder but a particularly sound opening bat and the perfect foil to my more risky aggression. The fact we knew each other I think gave us the confidence not only to cope with the occasion but also the rather competent opening attack of Paul Goodwin from Lancing and Graham Roope. Philip looked immoveable while I got enough loose deliveries to keep the scoreboard ticking along nicely. We'd put on 98 together in 80 minutes of which I'd scored 68 when a most embarrassing incident occurred. I was waiting to receive the next delivery when blood started pouring from my nose, liberally splattering the back of my bat and that holy of holies the Lord's pitch. Luckily Harry Sharp, the umpire, saw I was in trouble and stopped the bowler in his tracks. By now I must have looked like a zombie wandering around with head thrown back, gloves, bat and cap flung in all directions, frantically searching for a handkerchief to help stem the flow. In these days of Health and Safety strictures doubtless an army of qualified medics would have been instantly at my side ready to stretcher me off to the nearest A & E, but in those days no such interest. Harry, after checking the holy of holies hadn't been too badly stained, proffered the imaginative suggestion that perhaps I ought to go off so they could get on with the game. So I staggered back to the Pavilion hardly seeing where I was going with the blood showing no inclination to stop. After ten minutes back in the dressing-room a selector appeared to see if I was all right and suggested a cold compress, not that he had one to offer. By then the bleeding had stopped but I wasn't exactly feeling great so it was agreed I could continue my innings in the morning. My little scene was regarded as a minor inconvenience and life, and the game, continued their sweet ways. We closed on 156 for three with Philip out for an excellent 47.

The next morning I felt fine and if there was still a touch of embarrassment when I returned to the crease after the fall of the fourth wicket, it was quickly suppressed with a glance up at the scoreboard which with astonishing speed and accuracy replaced the departed no. 4 with a no. 1 and 68 next to it. Obviously there's a hell of a thrill batting at Lord's, but it's even better when you go in fresh with 68 already on the board! So I was full of confidence and the runs seemed to come quickly and easily, although I was dropped off a difficult chance in the gully. I've never really been nervous in the nineties, which probably explains why I often got out in them, and when on 94 I drove the off-spinner Roger Davis through the covers in successive balls, first for 4 and then for 3, the magic three figures went up on that famous old Grandstand scoreboard. I was out not long after for 108 but a hundred at Lord's! Unbelievable! It's there, in Wisden, as proof! And it can't be taken away! I have to go on about it as it was downhill ever thereafter! Perhaps the best part was that dear old EWE from Heath Mount days was there to see the moment, and he was so obviously pleased and proud when we had a chat at the end of the day. For the first time I began to appreciate the rewards of schoolmastering.

The innings ended on 262 with only Pat Neate getting a decent score with 33. Rupert Daniels returned the impressive figures of 5-50 with his off-spin. Time was running out to get a decent game and the selectors made it clear they wanted to see as much as possible of those who hadn't shone to-date. The Southern Schools moved rapidly to 128 for five before declaring leaving us 201 to get in just over 150 minutes.

Our batting order was juggled around to give everyone a chance but only Philip Spray (48) and Roger Tolchard (39) impressed. When the ninth wicket went down on 142 with a quarter of an hour left, I joined Phil Carling at the crease and together we saw the day out to get the draw.

This year I knew I'd be in the final Schools' XI to play the Combined Services over the next two days. Rupert was to be the captain and I was vice. Philip Spray was selected which was great as was someone I knew from the Essex Y.A., Mike Edmonds. It was a strong side particularly in the batting with plenty of variety in the bowling, and we all had the thrill of two more days playing at Lord's, this time, though, not in a trial, but in a serious competitive match against experienced adults.

*

SOUTHERN SCHOOLS v. THE REST

Tuesday & Wedsday, August 4 & 5, 1964   (2-day Match)

SOUTHERN SCHOOLS

		First Innings		Second Innings	
1 G. R. J. Roope	............Bradfield	b Spray	32	--------------------------	
2 M. J. Edmonds	...City of London	l b w b Elviss	24	l b w b Spray	41
3 D. R. Aers	.................Tonbridge	c Tolchard b Elviss	83	not out	16
4 R. C. Constant	............Sherborne	c Neate b Grimsdick	2	c Chapman b Elviss	13
†5 R. C. Daniels	......................Eton	hit wicket b Grimsdick ..101		--------------------------	
6 N. C. D. Craig	...........Winchester	c Neate b Chapman	5	b Spray	16
7 J. M. M. Hooper	......Charterhouse	not out	51	not out	26
8 J. L. Hutton	..................Repton	c Tolchard b Grimsdick..	0	c Tolchard b Neate	7
9 R. C. Davis	........................Blundell's	not out	31	--------------------------	
*10 D. W. W. Norris	............Harrow	--------------------------		c Grimsdick b Spray......	0
11 P. R. Goodwin	...............Lancing	Innings closed		Innings closed	
		B , l b 2, w 1, n-b 2,	5	B 4,1-b 5, w , n-b ,	9
		Total	334	Total 128	

FALL OF THE WICKETS

1—44   2—97   3—110   4—184   5—207   6—262   7—262   8—   9—   10—
1—26   2—61   3—72   4—72   5—99   6—   7—   8—   9—   10—

ANALYSIS OF BOWLING

Name	1st Innings						2nd Innings				
	O.	M.	R.	W.	Wd.	N-b	O.	M.	R	W	Wd. N-b
Neate..........................	13	5	20	0	1	...	8	2	19	1	... ...
Marks	5	2	12	0	...	...	5	1	15	0	... ...
Spray..........................	9	3	32	1	...	2	9	1	30	3	... ...
James	3	0	24	0	...	...	7	0	38	0	... ...
Grimsdick	19	3	75	3	...	...	4	1	12	0	... ...
Elviss..........................	31.3	4	98	2	...	...	4	1	5	1	... ...
Chapman	19	3	68	1	...	...	...	...	...	...	... ...

THE REST

		First Innings		Second Innings	
†1 N. J. Chapman	...............Felsted	c Norris b Edmonds 108		not out	5
2 P. H. Spray	...................Bedford	b Daniels	47	c Edmonds b Davis	48
3 D. C. Haywood	.........Notts. High	c Hutton b Daniels	10	c Constant b Aers	2
4 C. P. Marks	..................Worksop	l b w b Daniels	0	b Davis	5
5 P. W. Neate	.................St. Paul's	c Norris b Roope	33	c Davis b Aers...............	0
6 A. B. Trentham	...............Rugby	b Goodwin	4	b Davis	4
*7 R. W. Tolchard	............Malvern	c Roope b Edmonds	9	l b w b Aers..................	39
8 A. R. G. James	.........Uppingham	c Norris b Daniels	2	b Daniels	6
9 R. W. Elviss	......Leeds Grammar	b Goodwin	12	c and b Edmonds	5
10 P. G. Carling	........Kingston G. S.	c Hooper b Daniels	5	not out	9
11 J. M. H. Grimsdick	.Merch't Tay's	not out	0	b Goodwin	0
		B 20, l b 11. w 1, n-b ,	32	B 22. l-b 4, w , n b 1,	27
		Total	262	Total	150

FALL OF THE WICKETS

1—132   2—147   3—151   4—170   5—188   6—234   7—235   8—247   9—256   10—262
1-2   2—75   3—95   4—107   5—112   6—113   7—114   8—133   9—142   10—

ANALYSIS OF BOWLING

Name	1st Innings						2nd Innings				
	O.	M.	R.	W.	Wd.	N-b	O.	M.	R.	W.	Wd. N-b
Goodwin	24.1	5	68	2	1	...	13	3	31	1	... 1
Roope	15	7	29	1	...	...	6	1	23	0	... ...
Aers	11	3	26	0	...	...	12	4	32	3	... ...
Davis	8	1	17	0	...	...	15	4	32	3	... ...
Edmonds	11	1	40	2	...	...	2	2	0	1	... ...
Daniels.........................	21	5	50	5	...	...	4	2	5	1	... ...

Umpires— H. P. Sharp & T. W. Higginson   Scorer—A. Fowler

† Captain   * Wicket-keeper

Play begins at 11 each day   Stumps drawn 1st day 7, 2nd day at 6.30 or 7

Luncheon Interval 1.30 p.m.—2.10 p.m.

Tea Interval 4.15 p.m.—4.35 p.m. (may be varied according to state of game)

Southern Schools won the toss

45

There was an air of eager expectancy when we all gathered in the Visitors' dressing-room the next morning but that changed to curiosity once Rupert returned from the toss. 'They've put us in,' he said, 'and it looks a pretty good track to me.' Good track or not, some seventy minutes later we were reeling on 48 for six. I'd opened with Graham Roope and we'd started well putting on 18 in no time before we were both out in quick succession for 9. Our much vaunted batting line-up then collapsed and it took the combined efforts of Mike Edmonds (16), Philip (54) and Roger Tolchard (34), all of whom batted extremely well in difficult circumstances, to bring some respectability to the innings. We were all out by mid-afternoon for 177, a poor score but infinitely better than it might have been.

The bowlers then made amends and aided by some superb fielding reduced the Services to 139 for six, and even that was due to a fifth wicket stand of 104 between Cpl. Mungre, a Jamaican serving in the RAF and Capt. Williams of the Army. I managed to cling onto two slip catches, one of which a Press Association photo sadly revealed to the world as being lodged between my elbow and chest. Mike Hooper ran out one of their openers with a superb stop in the covers, then throwing down the wicket at the bowler's end. I had a decent spell getting a couple of wickets, one of which came from that old favourite of the leg-spinners' union, the undisguised long-hop. It pitched marginally closer to the batsmen than to myself, turned gently to the off and sat up invitingly. Lt. Moylan-Jones, RN, who had just come in, could hardly believe his luck, especially as the leg-side Grandstand boundary was temptingly close. He swivelled in his crease and whacked the ball with all his might, connecting right in the middle of the bat. By rights he should have been looking to clear Father Time, but I suppose in the Navy with all that deck cricket, you train yourself to avoid aerial shots. Even so it was still rising as it passed over Nick Craig at mid-wicket. Now Nick is not a particularly tall chap, rather more rotund and shapely, a wicket-keeper normally and, like all, well most, Wykehamists, a lovely chap to boot. Somehow in the split second available he managed to take off, stretch his right arm up and pluck the ball out of the air. It was a most sensational catch and one that almost caused the master i/c cricket at Winchester to fall off the Pavilion balcony. The Navy withdrew disbelievingly and the scorecard read Lt. R.Moylan-Jones c Craig b Chapman 0. Looks good to me! And who's not going to think it wasn't a devilishly good ball, viciously zipping off the pitch, just catching the outside edge and being caught comfortably at slip ... the unplayable ball?

But all that happened before the big partnership. At the close though we had got ourselves back in the game and things were evenly balanced. The next morning we got three quick wickets before the Services declared on 153. They obviously fancied a chase.

I again opened the batting with Graham and we were both probably at our best. In the words of the Telegraph correspondent: 'There was a great deal to admire in the batting of Roope and Chapman, who put on 110 for the Schools' first wicket in 95 minutes. They both had so much time to play the ball and there should be a future in the game for these two.' Got one right there anyway! I got 59 and Graham 70 and we were so well supported with speedy cameos after, not least Nick Craig's 37, that Rupert was able to declare on 201 for six, leaving the Services 226 to win at 90 an hour.

When their fourth wicket fell on 113 with just over 70 minutes left it looked as though we were in for a close finish. It was close time-wise but sadly we failed to capture another wicket as Messrs. Mungre and Williams again despatched us all around the famous ground. They reached their target with two minutes to spare and we simply had to bow to a superb display of batting. But it had been a great game.

There was one particularly interesting moment during that last day. As always at Lord's there were a lot of famous people wandering about in the Pavilion and you sensed your behaviour was being monitored from the moment you stepped through the well-defended portals. I had just got out in the second innings and had collapsed onto one of the sofas in the dressing-room to remove the various impedimenta of batting, tired and disappointed to have got out but pleased to have batted well, when a huge man marched in and made straight for Rupert, who was padding up at the far end of the room. In a deep, sonorous voice, he boomed: 'Daniels, you've had a magnificent season, many congratulations and the very best of luck next year up at Oxford.' Rupert, of course, leapt to his feet (I was mildly surprised that he neither bowed nor saluted), and replied with a 'Thank you very much indeed, Sir.' The vast frame then glowered down at me and strode out of the room. We were all agog. Who was this Great Man? Rupert of course knew and revealed to our amazement that it was E.W. Swanton. None of the rest of us had recognised him at all despite having seen him umpteen times on the tele. It was the sheer size of the man that threw us, I suppose. And there was an aftermath, inevitably, as Chapman had not leapt to attention. The Great Man had lunch that day in the Old Tavern, and doubtless his companions were also great men, when he was asked his opinions of the current crop of schoolboys on show.

EWS announced loud and clear: 'Daniels will go far. Great potential. Lovely chap. Chapman. He's a bit cocky.' Unfortunately my mother was on the neighbouring table and it was all my father could do to stop her belting EWS over the head with her handbag. Sadly she was not good at keeping such delicate comments to herself, so put out was she, and my wretched brother labelled me with that soubriquet thereafter.

There was another call from Harry Altham to play in his XI v ESCA the following week. It was a dour game unfortunately and I didn't distinguish myself. Including such prodigies as Graham Johnson and Trevor Jesty they scored 217 for four rather too slowly and left us considerably less time. Harry made it clear we had to go for them but we finished on 197 for seven, the unbeaten eighth wicket putting on 45 to make it look respectable.

Of the 1964 Schools' XI three went on to make a mark in first-class cricket – Graham Roope for Surrey and England, Roger Tolchard for Leicestershire and England, Mike Hooper for Surrey. The rest of us played at more modest levels but I suspect just as, if not more, enjoyably. Over two years, I'd played ten days cricket at the most famous ground in the world, an experience for which I've remained forever grateful and will never forget.

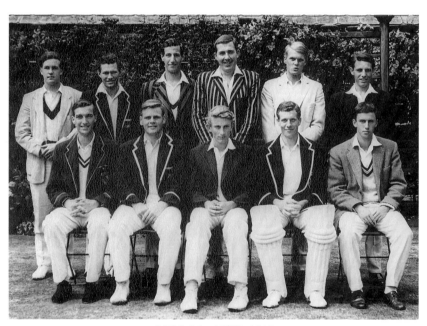

MCC Schools' XI, 1964
Nick Craig, David Aers, Mike Edmonds, Richard Elviss, Mike Hooper, Roger Tolchard
Paul Goodwin, Nigel Chapman, Rupert Daniels, Graham Roope, Philip Spray

5. ESSEX

It was the summer of '66 and I had been given the term off teaching so I could play cricket full time. I had by now played several times for Essex 2nd XI and thought let's give it a go for a whole season, and see what happens. The previous autumn I had written to Trevor Bailey, the doyen of Essex cricket, secretary and captain, to ask whether he'd be prepared to let me be with the county for the coming summer and he'd kindly replied to say that he'd be delighted as long as I realised that they would only be able to pay my expenses, there was no way they could afford wages for extra players. I fully appreciated this as Essex at the time were in a parlous state financially, with no home base and a squad of just 11 or 12 full time professionals. From my point of view it was now or never and at age 20 it was arguable I had already left it a bit late. I was told to report to the Indoor School in Ilford early in April.

It was an interesting experience. The first session was a lengthy one as all the pros had a decent stint with the bat and it was clear my bowling, quite rightly, didn't merit much consideration. I knew several of the younger players from the 2nd XI games and there was some good banter. When the day ended and I hadn't had a bat, they said not to worry it was always a bit like that to start with and my turn would come. The Chief, as Trevor Bailey was known, had barely been seen. He'd eased himself through a few overs and a brief go with the bat before retiring to his secretary's office near the entrance. He summoned me in as I was about to go merely to confirm that I'd be paid expenses only, but would get £15 for any game I played in the 1st team, which was encouraging to think that he'd even considered it a possibility. Next day, he said, report to Fairlop for some outdoor nets.

Next day though was wet so it was more of the same indoors. Frank Rist, an occasional 1st team wicket-keeper, and now 2nd XI coach/manager, appeared in the afternoon and I hinted to him it might be an idea if I had a bat, so he arranged for a couple of the other hangers-on to stay behind to bowl. We eventually got outside the next week but due to the conditions only the senior batsmen got into the nets and most of the time was spent on fielding practice. Thanks to the dreadful weather, we were at Fairlop for just a couple of days and then 'pre-season' seemed to disintegrate. There was a day at Fenner's when, thanks solely to Gordon Barker, I had that valuable batting session in the nets already mentioned, a few Club and Ground fixtures when Frank Rist raised an

XI to face a club team and that was it, before we were unleashed to play the other county sides invariably packed with pros in the Second Eleven Championship.

Gordon Barker with his three England protégés
Nick Knight, Gordon Barker, Derek Pringle, John Stephenson

*

Surrey were a case in point. They would always put out seven or eight full time pros, most of whom you'd heard of, and fill the side up with young trialists fighting like mad to earn a contract. We were simply a hotch-potch of reasonably good club cricketers who happened to be at the end of the phone when Frank rang round trying to fill up his team and with the exception of Keith Boyce there was rarely a pro. (Keith had famously been 'discovered' by The Chief on a trip to Barbados and was now in the second of two years qualifying before being eligible to play for the county.) On this particular occasion amidst their usual array, Surrey had decided to play one G.G. Arnold. I'm not entirely sure why he was playing as he was by this stage a regular in the first team and his name had been mentioned for a possible England call-up. Perhaps he had been injured and was regaining fitness, perhaps he fancied some cheap wickets. In official circles he was described as fast-medium, but to us rabbits in the Essex dressing room he was decidedly faster than fast. It would not take long for us to find out as perhaps foolishly we elected to bat first.

As one of Frank's 'regulars' I was batting at 4 but had barely got my pads on before the first wicket fell, shortly followed by a huge appeal to indicate that the Horse had struck again in his second over. My presence was required rather earlier than expected at the crease. Sadly this meant I was denied any gems of advice that Frank might have been able to proffer about how to play this famous bowler. Never mind, I thought as I took guard, it's probably better to find out for oneself.

The first problem was rather an alarming one. I couldn't see the great man. All seemed ready, but there was no bowler, or at least not that I could see. The somewhat rotund and solidly built umpire then announced that he was coming around the wicket, 'he' being this highly tuned, slim, super fit athlete who I now realised had been hidden from view by the substantial figure of the said official. Obviously the great GG had been thrown when he saw I was a left-hander and been forced to adjust his run-up. One up to me, I chuckled to myself ... he may be famous but clearly hasn't done his homework! I must be in with a chance!

The second problem was of course that I couldn't see his approach to the wicket until the very last second, hidden as he was by the considerable bulk of the umpire. So for a second or so as I settled at the crease there was a mild concern as to whether he was approaching at all. I needn't have worried as with a great rush of wind and a whirling of arms he suddenly appeared and unleashed the ball in my direction.

Remarkably I saw it. I had thought it was possible he would be so fast that the ball would be past before I realised, but, no, I could see it clearly, very clearly. In fact if I had had to track each nano-second of the delivery I could have done so. It even crossed my mind (in a nano-second) that this reputation lark was all tosh. Here was one of England's most promising fast bowlers and I could see the ball. Easy. In fact it was a seemingly fairly ordinary delivery. Fast, yes; but not that fast. It was well outside my off stump. A good length, as was only to be expected. Clearly, as my highly tuned batsman's brain intimated, a ball to leave well alone. So I placed my right foot down the wicket outside the off stump, and nonchalantly raised my bat into the air to usher the ball past, to indicate not just to one G.G. Arnold but also to all these professional fielders that here was a batsman to be reckoned with. He knew his stuff. He could play.

The third, and final, problem was that the ball then did something totally unexpected. It swung. Dramatically. And late. The word 'viciously'

51

springs to mind. And, sadly, in. It was as though that ball had some kind of homing device to take it past my pad and then veer sharply to the left. It crashed into my off stump which, to add further indignity, cartwheeled almost into the wicket-keeper. I couldn't believe it. I stood there and gaped. Firstly at the missing stump. Then secondly at the bowler, who showing no surprise or elation whatsoever had already turned to prepare for the next incompetent novice.

I slunk off back to the pavilion and en route had to pass Mike Hooper at cover who had played in the same Schools' XI at Lord's two years earlier. "Bad luck, Nige," he said, "probably not the right ball to leave!"

Somehow or other we scraped together 81 runs, extras being the second highest scorer with 13. The famous bowler returned the impressive figures of 9 overs 5 maidens 16 runs 6 wickets. We wondered whether he had ever had it easier. The first innings of the 2nd XI Championship in those days was restricted to 55 overs and we had used exactly half of the allotted number. Surrey inevitably used their full amount, but only reached 172 for seven before the enforced declaration, thanks to lengthy and impressive spells from John Lever and Ray East, so remarkably we weren't totally out of the game.

My next encounter with the great man was delayed somewhat longer in the second innings, and the score was well into the thirties before the second wicket fell. Now I had Frank's helpful advice ringing in my ears. "He bowls away swingers. In to you." Thanks, Frank. Luckily I was able to get off a pair by edging a couple to third man off the other opener before being obliged to face one G.G. Arnold again.

There were no initial alarms this time around. The umpires had changed ends and the tall, slimline beanpole had no chance of hiding the bowler, but I was on the lookout, I knew where he was. So as he came hurtling in around the wicket I had a few more split seconds mentally to prepare for the delivery. "He bowls away swingers. In to you." Our coach was spot on and I had the experience to know how correct he was.

The problem this time was that the ball was not on the off. This was annoying. I had planned my defence to the last millimetre, my feet and bat would be perfectly positioned to adapt to any amount of swing and ensure the off stump could not be hit. I had even anticipated the ball going straight on, as clever bowler as he clearly was, he could play that trick and I would not be found wanting. But this ball was angled across me, and clearly going down the legside. I didn't have any plan for this, but it obviously didn't matter. This was clearly an unintended delivery. And, dare one even mention it, a bad ball. I wouldn't even bother playing at it. It was possibly going to be a wide after it swung; if not, we could even get a bye. No worries!

The first moment of alarm came as the ball approached my legs. It wasn't swinging away as it should have done, but seemed to be holding its line, even, horror of horrors, starting to come back. I thought I had left my pad in line with the leg stump but in the highly tuned batsman's brain alarm bells started ringing furiously. Too late. The ball did the exact opposite to yesterday's, and in a panic I prodded at it as the homing device took it around my legs only to nick it straight into Derek Taylor's expectant gloves, and the pair triumphantly roared an appeal. I looked at the great G.G. Arnold who smiled sympathetically. For the second time in 24 hours I slunk off the field in ignominy. Mike Hooper simply managed a "Bad luck." I informed Frank that there was a bit more to GG than away swingers.

With me out of the way, the Essex innings began to prosper with Keith Boyce scoring a speedy 42 and then amusingly Ray East added an unorthodox 30-odd at the end for us to reach a respectable 202. Geoff Arnold merely managed 3-43 off 21 overs this time. Surrey required 112 to win.

Surprisingly they nearly made a hash of it. Graham Pritchard had one of his inspired sessions and bar a short break of three overs bowled unchanged getting 6 wickets. Ably supported by Ray East they had Surrey in a mighty panic and when Geoff joined Derek Taylor for the last wicket 4 runs were still required for victory. Inevitably, I suppose, he had the last laugh edging one past me at slip which really I should have stopped.

I never came across the great man again, merely read about him in the papers and watched him bowling for England and proudly thought 'I faced him once!' Yes! Two balls, two wickets! Some rabbit! The Cricketer Magazine profiled him at the height of his England fame and mentioned that at the time of writing he had still to get a hat trick. His nearest was for Surrey II v Essex II when he got two wickets in two balls and the man facing the hat trick ball was one young West Indian called Keith Boyce. He steered it straight to first slip who dropped a sitter.

Now that would have been a good story. Part of Geoff Arnold's only hat-trick! Who else was done? Oh, only Keith Boyce.

*

My two runs against Surrey came after a run of four consecutive ducks so marked an improvement! Even so, it was with no little surprise that a week or so later there was a call from Frank to say that I was needed urgently to travel with the 1st team to Bradford for the match with Yorkshire. Apparently Mickey Bear was indisposed and they needed batting cover. It was almost certain that I'd be 12th man but not impossible that I'd play. So I spent an entertaining afternoon playing pool with Graham Saville while we awaited the arrival of Barry Knight in his Mercedes for the lengthy trip north. On arrival at the hotel The Chief thanked me for coming and said that as the Bradford wicket was so seamer friendly he was inclined to play an extra batsman, but he'd make a final decision in the morning.

I don't know what made him change his mind, (probably a phone call to Frank to check on current form!), but next morning the decision was to play Ray East and I was to be 12th man. I was neither surprised nor that disappointed but was touched when both Robin Hobbs and Brian Edmeades said they were sorry I wouldn't be making my debut and hoped it would be soon. It epitomised the camaraderie and friendliness of the Essex dressing-room – I was barely part of the squad yet they made sure I felt included.

The changing room at Bradford was a curious affair as both teams shared the one large area, with the home side having the larger more comfortable half. The only view of the playing area though, was from the visitors end and I was soon subject to comment and curiosity when the Yorkshire players gathered to watch their team bat, not that it was easy with smoke billowing from Fred Trueman's pipe. The time seemed to speed by as they scored at more than four an over with Brian Close especially aggressive. Suddenly there was an ''ey lad, yer needed' as Barry Knight was hobbling off the field waving up to the dressing-room. I sped downstairs and forced my way through the packed Members' Enclosure onto the field and immediately felt rather lonely. Here was this large arena full of enemy supporters baying with delight at every boundary. And I was put at third man right in front of them! The next over though I was brought up to cover but even that was in the firing line as Close hammered the first two balls straight at me somewhat harder than I was used to. It didn't last long though as the regulations restricted the first innings to 65 overs, and Essex were soon in chasing a total of 263.

They had said that Fred Trueman was past his best, but no-one in the Essex team that day would subscribe to the theory. He turned in one of his very best performances with 8-37 off 23 overs and had us struggling to avoid the follow-on. Of course Trevor Bailey was in his element in such circumstances and he found a worthy partner in Tony Jorden as they put on 30 for the ninth wicket to just save the ignominy.

There was one incident of note earlier in the innings which was to have a sequel a month later, when he got his front teeth knocked out. Rodney Cass, a Yorkshireman playing for Essex, and a particularly determined and belligerent bat, was not going to be cowed by Fred. Largely due to his roots, I suspect, he came in for a bit of rough treatment, but when Fred dropped one a fraction shorter than usual, Rodney swivelled in his crease and hooked the ball magnificently over square leg for six. He certainly got the glare, and doubtless a choice remark or two, but it was noted in the memory bank. Rodney was soon out the other end which would have endeared him to Fred even more! In the return fixture on a drying wicket at Leyton, Fred took full advantage of the conditions and got one to rear up into Rodney's face. Brave man, he soldiered on, succumbing soon after without, again, giving Fred the satisfaction of getting his wicket.

Barry Knight bowled just one ball in the second innings and I was back on the field, which was a shame in a way as the comments in the dressing-room would have been interesting. But it was not a long stint as Yorkshire declared on the second evening leaving Essex with the near impossible target of 261 for victory.

As I'd be unused on the final day, I asked The Chief if he'd consider releasing me to play in the 2nd XI game that was due to start the next morning at Chelmsford. He readily agreed, said he'd ring Frank to confirm it, gave me the money for the train fare and by 8.00pm I was speeding my way back south.

I reported to the ground in good time only to be greeted by a bemused Frank:

"What are you doing here? You're meant to be in Bradford."

"Chief released me to play here today. Said he'd tell you."

"First I've heard of it. And I've had a terrible time getting eleven here. Can't let them down now. You can be 12th man if you want."

Thanks, Frank.

*

In those days the Single-wicket Competition was a highlight of the season. All the counties had their internal event, the winners of which progressed to Lord's for the Finals together with some international stars invited by the sponsors. There was no little money involved so it was a keenly contested affair, not least at county level where any reputable all-rounder felt he was in with a chance. In Barry Knight and Keith Boyce, Essex had two players more than capable of winning the national event so it was a significant day when 17 players gathered at Chelmsford to determine the Essex champion. Obviously all the pros were there together with four or five of the more regular 2nd XI players.

Among the latter were myself and Terry Dash, and we had been drawn to play each other in the one game in a preliminary round. Terry was a lovely chap, a rotund, friendly extrovert who invariably appeared at any match with a tray full of apples, plums or other fruit from his farm. And at this level we certainly had one thing in common – we were as bad as each other. So the opening contest of the day should at least be closely matched ... and the winner would have the dubious honour of playing Keith Boyce in the first round proper.

Terry won the toss, and as was the norm, elected to field first. He bowled fairly innocuous off-spinners, marginally more dangerous than my eminently hittable leg-spin. He spread his first-class fielders far and wide, left a slip in together with a silly mid on and off. At this stage of the competition we were allocated four overs each, which was approximately three and a half more than Boycey would require to dispose of either of us.

The first ball was a short-pitched delivery on the leg stump, turning ever so gently to the off. I managed to push it past silly mid on into a large vacant area and yelled "Yes ... two." Immediately the whole field was convulsed in laughter and I was so confused that I did well to complete one before the ball came rocketing back to Tonker Taylor at the stumps. As I returned to the receiving end, Tonker politely pointed out that as I had no partner, no call was strictly necessary ... but they had enjoyed the moment and encouraged me to continue. I didn't.

The second ball was a juicy full toss outside leg which I smashed between the two fielders on the leg boundary. No running, or thankfully, calling, was required. Immediately I felt up for the job in hand and not even the spectre of Keith in the next round dimmed my confidence. The third ball was a juicy half-volley on the off allowing me to display my favourite shot, the off drive. I got my right foot to the ball and with a great flowing stroke gave it an almighty belt. Keith Fletcher, at silly mid off, plucked the ball up an inch off the ground and nonchalantly lobbed the ball back to Terry with a casual aside "Well ... this won't take long." I was out. For 5. To Terry Dash. I'd have been proud of 5 against Boycey ... but to Terry! He couldn't resist a grin as we went into the shed that served as the pavilion in those days to change roles ... "It's so much easier when you've got decent fielders, it's what I've been missing all season!"

How do you defend 5 ... as a leggie? I set out my 'attacking' field, with only a deep square on the boundary, a slip and a ring saving one either side of the wicket. Mr Dash was going to have to lift it over the top to get his runs. He knew what I bowled so I opened with the googly. The googly that was so easily spotted by any moderately competent schoolboy. But Terry was possibly a tad nervous batting amidst such exalted fieldsmen and with Tonker breathing down his neck ... "juicy cherry here, Terence, my old fruit"... completely misread it and got an inside edge. Straight to Tonker, who probably still pleased with his bon mot, also, amazingly and confoundedly, misread it and dropped it. "Sorry, Nigel." "No worries, Brian. You're bound to get another chance."

Two dot balls followed. The tight field was putting pressure on. If only I can keep it on a length, Dashy might get himself out. The next ball showed variation and imagination. My faster one, with a touch of off spin that invariably meant it went straight on. But the damn thing was just short of a length. Terry stepped back and prepared to cut it viciously through the close-set off side field. But he got it wrong. Perhaps the ball was quicker than he thought, perhaps it kept a bit low, either way he misjudged it, got a bottom edge, straight into Tonker's gloves ... and out again! He didn't apologise this time, just shook his head disbelievingly. Clearly he'd never had to keep to such idiosyncratic bowling in his life before. Fortunately he never had to do so again. The next two balls were the inevitable long hops which Terry smashed to the boundary. Game over.

At least I was spared the terror of facing Boycey in the next round. Terry won the toss and inserted the famous West Indian who merely scored 49* in his four overs. Terry lasted three balls, two whistling past his chin and the third removing his off stump. There but for the grace of God ...

I spent the rest of the day fielding for about half of the matches and admiring Keith Boyce's inevitable progression through to the final where he lost out to Barry Knight. Barry sadly didn't repeat his success of two years earlier at Lord's, losing this time in the second round, surprisingly to Keith Stackpole. Boycey though didn't have to wait long as he triumphed in 1969.

*

I had one other game as 12th man for the 1st XI, at Leyton, after one afternoon of which I received a frantic phone call from a friend at home. "I saw you on the field against Glamorgan today ... were you playing ... have you made your debut?" Sadly I had to disappoint him, and it was not to happen. It would have been nice to say you'd played for Essex, but it would have been one or two games at the most which isn't the real thing. I had neither the ability nor the temperament to succeed at that level and the lack of resources within Essex at the time meant I was unlikely to improve. E.W. Swanton made an apposite comment in his weekly column in the Telegraph soon after one of the representative schools' games at Lord's when, commenting on the number of the players who had already been selected for county 2nd XIs, he wrote: 'I think the benefit to the boy depends on how the particular second XI is run ... if there is any doubt, these young cricketers would be better off playing the best club cricket.'

He was probably right, but I still had a highly enjoyable summer.

6. THE ROBINS

One of the most enjoyable forms of the game in those days was Old Boys' cricket. It certainly wasn't the highest standard, although some of it could be very good judging by the number of first-class and minor counties players who frequented it from time to time. The pleasure came I suspect from playing with people you knew who had the same philosophy about the game. It avoided the worst excesses of League cricket which was to become increasingly popular, but it lacked the intensity of the latter. In the early 1970s, the better players who were so inclined could opt for a League game on a Saturday and play in the more leisurely 'wandering' cricket on the Sunday, but even that became difficult as the Leagues and fixtures proliferated over time.

Thanks to the enthusiasm of one Old Boy in particular, Jamie Keep, the Old Felstedians did have a handful of games each summer usually on a Sunday against club sides in Essex. John Cockett also ran a cricket week back at the school after the end of term which had inevitably the same sort of ethos about it and although his sides invariably included several Old Boys, especially recent leavers, he often included members of staff and other cricketing friends, so it was correctly referred to as his XI. But no O.F. Cricket Club as such existed.

Thanks to the inspiration of two particularly keen wandering cricketers, Tony Winlaw and Henry Lewis, soon to be joined by Ben Brocklehurst of 'The Cricketer', an Old Boys' knockout competition was started in 1967, comprising 16 of the better known public schools. It was in fact the first of a number of club knockout competitions that soon became a focal part of amateur cricket over the next decade. Understandably Felsted was not included in the initial 'Cricketer Cup', as it was to be called, but we were particularly keen not to be left out when the competition was increased to 32 schools, as was rumoured to be happening fairly soon.

It was with this in mind, together with the wish to increase the number of regular O.F. games, that in April 1967 I wrote to the four people most closely involved in our cricket: Jamie Keep and John Cockett obviously, but also Roger Luckin who had played some 20 times for Essex and was by some way our best player, and most significantly to my great friend and exact contemporary Martin Foster. He and I went a long way back as our holiday matches started when we were 8 or 9 and were keenly contested although for reasons I found hard to fathom at the time his side invariably won. We were then in the same teams at Felsted and for five years his wicket-keeping made my leg-spinners look far better than they really were. The letter proposed the formation of an O.F. Cricket Club with various suggestions as to how we should go about it, and not least that our very existence could only strengthen our chances of being invited to join this exciting new Cup competition. Martin's reply came by return, right behind the idea, the others soon after with the result that we all met up on Whitsunday and created the Club. I was to be the Secretary, Martin the Treasurer and Jamie the Fixture Secretary. I was keen we should have a more enigmatic name than just 'Old Felstedian Cricket Club' which seemed to me to be rather boring. John Cockett, who was the real doyen of Felsted cricket and to whom we all owed so much, had recently had a son who was christened Robin, so I suggested 'Felsted Robins Cricket Club'. This would enable John's huge contribution to Felsted cricket to be forever linked with the Club, as well as giving the sort of friendly image that epitomised Felsted and the way we played our cricket.

And so the Felsted Robins were born. In 1968 we had 20 fixtures on our inaugural list and in 1969, by which time Sam Luckin, Roger's brother, had taken over the Fixture Secretary's role from Jamie, there were 29. All the original O.F. games had been embraced by the Club, John had added the seven games of his week, but the most significant and pleasing date on that card was Sunday, May 25 v Charterhouse Friars (H), in the first round of the newly expanded Cricketer Cup. We were in!

*

It was one thing to be in the competition but there were some very good sides involved and somehow we had to justify our inclusion. The last thing we needed to do was to make fools of ourselves. We were reasonably confident as in our part of the world we held our own against some strong club sides, but this was going up a notch. The draw against Charterhouse conjured up images of P.B.H. May coming to play on The Front, not to mention Richard Gilliatt, already established in the Hampshire team, but as it happened on the day neither appeared. Charterhouse had instead merely five who had played at first-class level, as against our one. We were going to have to be at our best, but at least we were at home.

Roger Luckin won the toss and unsurprisingly elected to bat. I opened once again with Doug Smith and together we quickly had 20 up, which was especially pleasing as Mike Hooper of those Lord's games had opened the bowling. But then disaster struck. I pushed the ball between mid-wicket and mid on and called Doug for what I thought was a straightforward single. Mid-wicket, confound him, swooped onto the ball panther-like and threw down the stumps at the bowler's end. I was out for a paltry 6. 21 for one became 21 for two as Doug was caught in the slips soon after for 13. Roger Luckin and Roger Nokes took the score albeit slowly to 48 before our skipper was caught for 10. Thereafter they seemed to have us in a stranglehold. Their captain, a giant of a creature, Anthony Allom, who at 6' 9" was rumoured to have been the tallest person who had played first-class cricket, bowled superbly well, very straight just short of a length conceding just 12 runs off 9 overs and he was well backed up by Ted Jackson's 4-21 off 10. Roger Nokes held the innings together with a brave 58 but 48 for three eventually became 114 for nine. Algy Rice our no. 11 hit out to become only the fourth to reach double figures and make our total 129, but it was a pitiful effort. We had singularly succeeded in making fools of ourselves.

Charterhouse certainly thought so as when we came out to field we heard a couple of them in earnest discussion with the captain about going back to London early, they clearly wouldn't be needed, the game would be over soon after tea, it was all rather a waste of time. It did cause us to think, that maybe … just maybe … if they were already counting some chickens …

Whatever … we at least bowled and fielded like demons and made them fight for every run. We were taking wickets regularly, but not regularly enough. That 129 was just too small a total and when we took their sixth wicket on 96 we thought there might be a chance, but Andrew Barker was still there with 40 not out and clearly had the match under control. The score crept up ever so slowly but with a certain inevitability. Roger, knowing all too well that our fifth bowler who would have to complete seven overs, was a weak link, decided to bowl out the four main ones, all of whom had been magnificent.

On 113, Martin Christy who played for the RAF, got one of his in-duckers to move away just that little bit more to the left-handed Andrew Barker and Martin Foster gleefully snapped up the chance behind the stumps, and their no. 3 was gone for an excellent 51. Seven down.

It was now that the atmosphere around The Front came into its own. There had been a fair number of spectators for the game anyway but the joy that greeted that vital wicket brought the boys out of their Houses and soon the driveway that surrounds the field in front of that huge

Victorian building was crowded with supporters cheering every dot ball and every run saved. The Common Room emptied out onto the drive, faces lent out of study windows, those comfortably ensconced in deck chairs had to get out and stand in order to see. Even the Headmaster came out of his front door to witness the dénouement. The Felsted community was now as one, pressurizing the opposition.

The Front at Felsted

The trouble was that at no. 9, Charterhouse had Ted Jackson who often batted three for Brondesbury, the powerful West London club. He started slowly, nudging the odd single here and there, but didn't look in any trouble at all. Just the man to see them through. Tony Ekins, our opening fast bowler who played for Cambridgeshire, was in his twelfth and final over, and the score had reached 123. His last ball was one of the finest he could have bowled. Pitching on a length just outside the line of off stump, it hit the seam, shot between the bat and pad of the hapless no. 8 and shattered his stumps. The arena exploded. The noise was such that a tennis match being played on the courts behind the school had to be stopped so they could come and watch. 123 for eight. Seven to win. Two wickets.

Their wicket-keeper, Oliver Popplewell, was no. 10 and had played for Cambridge University so presumably could keep an end up. But he wasn't facing. Martin Christy had one over left and he was bowling to Ted. The first ball erred too much to leg and Ted glanced it to fine leg and called 'two.' Luckily Tony Ekins was down there and he wasn't the England hockey captain for nothing. He could move ... and he had a bullet-like throw. Oliver, sensible man, saw this and to huge cheers from the crowd, declined the second. 124 for eight.

Now there was pressure. Roger brought the field in to stop the single. He took his time. Adjustments were needed for the new man. The hubbub from the crowd subsided as Martin ran in. He was now swinging the ball consistently and this one was another beauty, a beast of a delivery to receive first ball. It was a bit quicker, dipped in as usual but bounced more than expected and caught the outside shoulder of the bat and flew through to Martin Foster who flung it in the air as the whole ground yelled an appeal. 124 for nine.

The noise and excitement were now at fever pitch. Whether the no. 11 could bat or not was largely irrelevant. Could he cope in this cauldron? And he had possibly four balls to face if he couldn't get off strike.

Ted met him some way from the wicket and goodness knows what he said as he walked him to the crease. Roger kept the field the same. Everyone was in on the one bar long leg and third man who were saving two. We knew we had ten balls to do it – Martin's four and Algy Rice's final over. He'd bowled his 11 overs for just 20 so he wouldn't give anything away. After that, we'd have to use not just a fifth but a sixth bowler ... and help! It suddenly dawned on me that that might mean me. The crowd were doubtless unaware of such intricacies as they fell silent once again as Martin started his run up.

I simply cannot remember that last ball. It is all a blur. I do remember the ground erupting as the stumps were shattered. People ran onto the field from all directions. Joy was unbounded. Such excitement, brought on by the unlikelihood and unexpectedness of it all, could hardly ever been seen on that lovely old ground before. I think initially we were slightly bemused. We'd won! By five runs, defending 129 on a jolly good batting track. It had seemed an impossibility. But in the cold light of reason they had batted no better than us – one fifty and only three others in double figures and the bowling figures were similar. Martin Christy finished on 11.3 overs, 26 runs, 4 wickets. Ted Jackson could only watch from the other end and was six not out. For the impartial observer, if such were present, it must have been a wonderful spectacle. It was a memorable occasion and an unforgettable game.

As usual we repaired to The Chequers next door. For the opposition it was too much and they speedily withdrew from the scene. Rightly or wrongly, that coloured my view of Carthusians for ever afterwards. We played them several times in later years, curiously always away, and generally were beaten very soundly. But we never declined to drink with them afterwards. As a schoolmaster I was obviously interested in the places we played and the people we played against, and was soon to discover that this competition did show up the ethos and character of a school in the way its representatives performed and behaved.

*

Sadly we fell in the second round three weeks later away to Brighton College. We lost by 11 runs, failing to chase down their modest total of 192 for nine, thanks largely to the self-inflicted indiscretion of six run outs.

The most frustrating consequence of this match, though, was that Brighton then went on to win the Cup, winning each of the three remaining rounds including the Final by over 100 runs. You need a bit of luck to win limited overs matches, but those margins suggest the opposition were outplayed. What a memorable year for them!

*

Over the years we had some marvellous games and played on some lovely grounds. One such occasion was at Tonbridge a few years after the Brighton farce. Colin Cowdrey played and it was a privilege to watch him bat from close quarters. There was a sort of majesty about him and he had so much time to play the ball. Anything off length or line was punished, not crudely or violently, but caressed or eased to the boundary accompanied by a sort of apologetic smile. But he treated each ball on its merits and as it happened we bowled rather well at him so he didn't score that fast and our big mistake was getting him out as it let in son Chris who was far more aggressive and their big hitting middle order who regularly drove the ball over the bowler's head for fours or sixes. But it was a great game as we fell just 10 short chasing their 240 odd. And they were their usual hospitable selves afterwards.

As were the Etonians who much to our consternation produced a case of gin after the game, and what's more it was finished. (This must have been before the days of the breathalyser!) Again, we'd lost but our 230 had been made to look horribly insignificant by Henry Blofeld who smashed over 50 in the first four overs. We were playing on Agar's Plough and some of his boundaries took a long while to retrieve, such is the size of the field. They just coasted home after his opening salvoes. Interestingly, this was the one and only occasion that I played against Johnny Barclay. I'm glad to say he didn't get his former teacher out, but my determination not to succumb to him probably led to my downfall at the other end after a breezy 30-odd.

Bradfield were fun to play in those days. Derek Pringle was available for one of these games and I found myself batting with him. Luckily he dealt mostly in boundaries as with his giant strides he could complete three runs in the time it took me to manage two. My demise must have left him wondering what he'd let himself in for. They had two Bodkins, both Doctors one of medicine, one of botany; the medic bowled left-arm spin and son Peter whom I knew well was the keeper. Trying to sweep a quicker ball behind square with the spin I toppled over, the ball hit Peter's right pad and ricocheted onto the stumps. By the time I gathered myself Peter was roaring with laughter, along with most of the fielders and the umpire, whose finger was raised. Chapman st Bodkin b Bodkin. Derek made no comment. He must have been relieved as he proceeded to score a century and win the match for us. At least I got two pints afterwards, one from each of the doctors, as I had clearly made their day.

But the side that made the biggest impression on me were the Shrewsbury Saracens. They were obviously a big name and a jolly good side. As it happened we played them three times in relatively quick succession. The first was on a rain-affected day at Felsted and we absolutely trounced them. They must have felt embarrassed, even humiliated, but there they were to a man in The Chequers afterwards with their guru, the inspirational Nicko Williams, leading the party. Two years later the boot was on the other foot and we were comprehensively dispatched on their ground. They'd laid on food and drinks in the pavilion afterwards and I think we repaid the compliment they'd shown us … at least Nicko's recollection of that evening was so hazy that we must have. Then the third game, again at Shrewsbury, was simply superb. Both sides scored around 240 and I can't remember who won. I think they did, but Nicko's not so sure. But in truth it didn't matter. It was such a good game that cricket and, in particular, The Cricketer Cup were the winners.

*

If that competition was the focal point of each Robins' season it certainly wasn't the raison d'etre of the Club. We, like all wandering sides, had trouble raising teams, particularly teams that were strong enough, but we fulfilled our fixtures, won most, lost enough, and in the process had an enormous amount of fun. There was a ready supply of new members from the school leavers each year and the Club flourished, as it still does today, if in a reduced capacity due to the demands of League cricket. Three Test cricketers are amongst our number with John Stephenson and Nick Knight joining the first, Derek Pringle.

I remained Secretary for 16 years when it was time to hand over to the younger generation. Martin and Sam continued in office for a bit longer to ensure continuity but they too then did the same. John Cockett ran the Cricketer Cup side for a number of years after he'd retired from teaching and he still takes a close interest in what's going on. He ran the cricket at Felsted for 29 years and his devotion to both the school and its cricket will forever be commemorated in the name of this Club.

7. COACHES ... COACHING

In April 1967 I went on a coaching course! A second summer toying with Essex would have been a waste of time and wasn't ever contemplated, and as Chris Snell had left Summer Fields the previous year, the post of master i/c cricket was vacant and I jumped at the opportunity to fill it. It occurred to me that much as I loved the game and really enjoyed playing it, I didn't have much of an idea of the technical side of coaching beyond common sense and my own experience of being coached.

I cast my mind over the five coaches who had shaped my cricketing career so far. Lyn Eardley (EWE) at Heath Mount instilled a love of the game and made it the greatest fun. He was very good on a one-to-one in a net and was very strong on the team ethic, but I was too young to appreciate whether he was talented as a coach. 'Mac' Gough, the Felsted pro was much stronger on specific and technical detail, but he had the time to spend with the individual, not least because he was being paid for it. Each half hour batting session with him was hard work as he flung balls at you until he was satisfied that each stroke was sufficiently well honed. He was gifted because he could spot what you were doing wrong and knew how to put it right. But, with the advantage of hindsight, he was teaching you to play on the Felsted wicket, his wicket, the one he spent hours preparing in his other capacity as groundsman. He taught me to play forward, to play straight and to drive and if you could do all those you would almost certainly score runs at Felsted. It took a long while to learn to adapt to other wickets and to learn to play off the back foot. He was intensely loyal to his school, and his charges, but I suspect had his limitations as a coach.

As it happened my first year in the lst XI saw 'Mac' replaced as coach by the old Essex pro Ray Smith. He had retired five years earlier but was still a famous name as he had been one of the most exciting and entertaining cricketers of his era, a mighty fine all-rounder with his dangerous swing/seam bowling and hard hitting lower order batting. We boys were thrilled such a distinguished cricketer was coming. (I heard much later that his Essex colleagues were amazed he'd taken up the position as they couldn't think of anyone less interested in nets, coaching and the technical side of the game.) His presence was an inspiration and his impact on fielding practices dramatic. He was a wonderfully friendly character to have around, did much for team spirit and was an especially good source of comfort if you were down. We all loved him. But from a technical coaching point of view he offered very little, in fact John Cockett, the master i/c, was a far better coach. I think the theory was that John would do the batting and Ray the bowling but in practice it wasn't so straightforward. John simply didn't have time for concentrated one-to-one net sessions and Ray found the 'teaching' aspect of coaching very difficult – a not uncommon problem for ex-pros. But their strength was that they got on so well together and John's forte was playing the game positively which fitted well with Ray's philosophy of the game. I suspect, though, we'd all have been much better players with a Gordon Barker around. I don't think it is a coincidence that no-one from this era went on to make a mark in the game.

The next 'coach' I came across was Frank Rist with Essex. To put it bluntly he simply wasn't a coach. He offered plenty of words of encouragement but very few of advice. In the middle of that summer of '66, when several of us were struggling, I had the temerity to ask him if he could organise some nets. His response was did I expect the 1st team players to come and bowl to me? No, I said, I didn't, but it might be sensible if we all turned up early before a 2nd XI match and had a net session with him. No, it would be too difficult to organise, with people having to take enough time off work as it was, he said. So I never ever had a net with him, nor saw him in a coaching role. But to be fair to him, it was the term that was wrong. He was really team secretary for the 2nds and Club and Ground XI and as such did noble service for the county. I suspect, too, he did it unpaid. Frank loved the game and loved Essex and was a wonderful servant to them. He got on with everyone, would chat away about cricket or football, invariably with a cup of tea in his hand and wouldn't have a bad word to say about anyone. I often popped into A.E. Sedgwick's, the sports store in Walthamstow where he worked, after an Arsenal game and there was always the warmest of welcomes. 'Hello, Nigel, great to see you! Have a cuppa! Good game?' You couldn't ask to meet a friendlier man. But he was no coach.

*

So here I was, aged 21, about to run a team for the first time, and my experience of coaches and coaching was somewhat limited. Those fifteen minutes with Gordon Barker had given me a frustratingly brief experience of what a naturally talented coach could do, but it looked as though I was going to have to learn on the job. A course was the obvious answer but this was in the days before such things became the norm. As it happened I was very lucky as the MCC were running a course for schoolteachers at Lilleshall, under the direction of Harry Crabtree, the recently appointed National Director of Coaching. Some 30 people had enrolled, of all ages, shapes and sizes. Several were obviously competent cricketers, many hardly played the game at all. Most were here voluntarily, some had clearly been sent by their schools. In addition to Harry, there were three fully qualified coaches to help run the course, two of whom were minor county cricketers, and the third, a schoolteacher, played to a high level in one of the Birmingham Leagues. We were soon divided up into four groups and as luck would have it I was allocated to Harry's group.

Harry sat us down and immediately made life difficult by asking us to think. This was clearly not going to be an ordinary net! He threw two questions at us. What do you want to get out of this course? What makes a good coach? Think about the second one, he said, while you're here and we'll discuss it in two days time. Meanwhile let's hear what you've got to say about the first.

We all seemed to have different answers. Someone wanted to get the basic qualification that was on offer, another wanted to learn how to teach a child to bowl, a third wanted ideas on fielding drills. I think I came up with some inane comment about how to use time in the nets most effectively for a whole group. Cleverly, he made us all feel that our answers were valid and to the point, and so with confidence boosted we started on the technical detail and how to hold the bat. Eight bats were laid out flat on the floor and we were told to imagine they were axes, pick them up and pretend to be chopping down a tree. Magically, with a few minor adjustments, even the three non-players in the group were holding a bat correctly. In turn, we then went to take up a batting stance with each having to correct someone else's grip where necessary. As I shaped up left-handed, Harry immediately said, 'Oh no you don't, you do all these exercises right-handed!' And of course I kept getting things wrong and quickly learnt the problems from a pupil's point of view. The other regular player in the group, a right-hander, was likewise made to do everything the wrong way round.

The two days passed in a flash, each session illuminated by some clever idea of Harry's as to how best to put over the particular coaching point of the moment. We were on the go the whole time, very little chat, all action coaching or being coached under his watchful eye, ever ready to help or pounce if we got something wrong. The best bit was learning to teach a beginner how to bowl and then progressing from the standing position to putting a run-up onto it. I was made to do it as a left-arm bowler, and my word, was it difficult! The poor chap having to coach me had a terrible time! But it was a brilliant way to learn how to coach. Harry was a real master of his art, and above all it was obvious we were all enjoying it.

On the second afternoon he had cunningly arranged for some local schoolchildren to appear for a coaching session from us students and all of us took turns in conducting net sessions, giving individual batting and bowling tuition and doing some fielding exercises, sadly all indoors due to the weather. It seemed to happen with clockwork precision as each child and each student did everything that was available, with no chance of being bored or inactive. It was clear a lot of planning and preparation had gone on beforehand, which was one of the clearest messages from the whole course.

For the final morning Harry quietly asked me to pad up and then proceeded to gather all the groups together. 'This is what is possible,' he said, and proceeded to chuck balls at me in a net shouting out ahead of each delivery what shot to play: 'cover drive', 'leg glance', 'square cut', 'back defence', 'straight drive for six', 'hook', etc and this went on for a shattering three or four minutes, until 'finally, drive through extra', which I decided to carve over cow corner which brought the house down followed by thunderous round of applause. I was not sure what this was meant to teach the others beyond a demonstration of the various shots, but I learnt an invaluable lesson. It was all very easy – because two of the hardest decisions a batsman has to make, had been made for me: determining the length of the ball, and what shot to play. Harry, of course, being a master of his art, threw each ball on to the perfect length for the shot he wanted to be played.

We then had an interesting discussion on what makes a good coach. Everyone had to contribute, and there were many sound and imaginative comments made. Harry summed up: 'All your ideas are valid and relevant of course, but none of you has mentioned the most important point of all. It doesn't matter at what level you coach, and naturally the higher the level the greater the technical knowledge required, but at whatever level, it's up to you to make it fun.'

He had certainly made it fun. He was a mighty fine coach of coaches.

*

Back at Summer Fields, I quickly came to realise that master i/c cricket was a somewhat bigger role than merely coaching the lst XI. You were responsible for running the game throughout the school and much of my time was spent organising fixtures, transport, kit, distribution of staff and so on. Luckily my organisational skills had always been quite good so that side of things took care of itself without too much difficulty but what with a full teaching timetable it was a struggle to prepare properly for the coaching of the lst team. This was clearly one of the reasons why the bigger schools employed full time coaches. No such luxury was possible in a prep school so inevitably individual coaching sessions became somewhat limited and one fell back on what John Cockett had been so good at, the team ethic, playing the game positively and ensuring it was fun for all involved.

I was lucky with the raw material available that year. Most of the boys could bat, one was especially promising, there were two decent fast bowlers and, joy of joys, two very competent spinners. David Dickson, the captain, was an offie, and James Parry a left-armer. This meant we were able to get through our overs at a fair rate.

We had a jolly good season, winning most, losing a couple and drawing very few. Most of the time we were on the attack and I like to think the team as a whole thoroughly enjoyed it. But from a coaching angle I can't honestly say I managed to improve any individual's skill level. Possibly the one general area that got better was the intensity of the fielding. By the end of term each boy was concentrating on each ball, imagining it was coming to him, whereas to begin with half the team found the fielding a chore and 'slept' through it. As proof, we caught some slip catches, which doesn't happen often at that age level, and got several run outs. But individual batting and bowling skills, no. I simply didn't have the ability in the time available to make a difference.

What I did learn was to get it all into perspective. Most of these kids would never play cricket at a serious level (there were no Johnny Barclays in this team!) and what they wanted more than anything was to enjoy the game. It was important to ensure they learnt to get their priorities right – cricket was important to them at school but it should not be the be all and end all.. It had meant too much to me at school to the extent my academic work suffered (with the wisdom of hindsight) but there was no danger of this being allowed to happen at Summer Fields, and my philosophy had to be in tune to the school's ethos.

Curiously, in all my 39 years teaching this was the only summer I was in charge of a lst XI. This was by coincidence rather than design in that I was away doing my degree for the next three years and on my return, as the person now running the cricket was well established, was asked to run the football which I wanted to do as I found it more interesting and challenging. It gave me scope to play more cricket but also led to running the Under 11 team for a number of years, before moving to the 2nd XI in my final years at the school.

I felt I really did make a difference with the ten year olds. Partially it was to do with more time being available as there was little admin to be concerned with, but more that technical coaching was required, simply because the children were younger. The enthusiasm was there in abundance but the experience inevitably limited. Obviously the level of coaching skills required was not high but it was tremendously rewarding to see the difference one's efforts made, and at that age improvement could happen quickly and dramatically.

The art was to keep it simple. We learnt to defend with a straight bat, and we leant to attack both with a straight and horizontal bat. We tried to keep the child's decisions to a minimum. Do I defend or attack this ball? Which of the five shots I've learnt do I use? With the bowlers we placed a towel in the nets and their job was to hit it. If they could do that once or twice an over we were getting somewhere, then we would try to spin or swing it according to what came naturally. It was all very basic and repetitive, as it needed to be, but the thrill for a boy when what he practised came off in a game made all the patience so rewarding.

The difficulty was controlling expectations. Not everyone could bat or bowl all the time so they had to learn to share responsibilities, in other words become part of a team, a big lesson in itself for the young. With the fielding, though, we were all involved all the time and to retain their attention I devised a scoring system whereby I kept a record of every run saved or lost and we posted a chart in the pavilion so they could see their progress. Eager eyes would be on me as I got out my notebook when umpiring to record a good stop and a huddle of boys would crowd around the chart whenever I was updating it to see who was in the lead for the fielding prize awarded at the end of the season. They loved it, and I have to confess, so did I.

The reward, too, was seeing boys one had trained up performing at a higher level a year or two later. If there was a particular star at Under 11 level, then I would always support his moving up early rather than get too many easy runs or wickets … provided he was going to get a bat or bowl at the higher level rather than just make up the numbers. In one of the first matches at this level, a boy, Peter Morris, scored a century and it was very obvious he was too good so he was immediately moved up and had three very successful years in the 1st team. He went on to play for Eton and later he even played with me a few times for North Oxford, so I think we got that one right!

*

There was still one more coach who was to make a great impression on me. Brian Edrich joined the staff at St Edward's, Oxford in 1964 as cricket professional following a moderately successful career in the game with Kent and Glamorgan. For a few years he continued playing for Oxfordshire and I first came across him when he was invited to help oversee some winter nets with the county in the early '70s. He was a left-handed batsman so immediately had an affinity with my weaknesses. Several times he took me aside for individual sessions in particular to straighten up my leg-side weight problems and to pass on his experience of how to determine the line on and just outside the off stump, a perennial nightmare for left-handers. Here was clearly someone with a natural gift for coaching, probably all the more so because he hadn't had the easiest of times in the first-class game. He was quick to spot a problem, had the technical expertise to show you how to put it right, and the patience to work at it with you. I felt he made a real difference to my batting, and as a teacher and coach myself now, could appreciate his skills all the more.

I think the best coaches are those who have played the game and are coaching at a level that is below the standard they reached as a player. It means you fully bring to bear on your charges the experience you had as a player. It implies you have the necessary technical know-how. An ability to teach is important too and for most schoolmasters this aspect is not a difficulty, but for the non-teacher, like most professional players, this is a skill they have to learn. Nowadays there are some excellent courses that fulfil this function, leading to various levels of qualification. But I believe the best teachers are natural, which is why for me, Harry Crabtree, Gordon Barker and Brian Edrich stood out as coaches of the highest calibre.

'Mac' Gough

Brian Edrich

Harry Crabtree

Frank Rist

8. NORTH OXFORD

In the autumn of 1970 I returned to Oxford to teach at Summer Fields, having completed my degree at Ealing Technical College, as an external student of London University. I had made it clear to Pat Savage, a lovely man who was still the Head, that I had no expectation of having the role of master i/c cricket back. In fact, if there was a chance, I'd far rather help with junior cricket teams in the hope that I could have Saturdays off in the summer so I could play some serious cricket myself while I was still young enough to do so. Pat agreed immediately, so the search for a club began.

By pure chance, the old school secretary, a wizened and friendly man called Eric Bowtell, still had connections with the school and was also closely involved with North Oxford C.C. He said that was the club for me to join as its founder some 70 years earlier had been the then Headmaster of Summer Fields, Dr Williams. An added advantage was their ground, the St John's College ground, was close by, just off the Woodstock Road. He would speak to the people he knew on the committee and see what could be done. The outcome was that in March the next year I had a phone call from the captain, Richard Pineo, inviting me to join them for nets when they started in April and also to play in their first game of the season which was a sort of internal trial/practice match when 22 members would get their first chance of an outing in the middle.

Luckily, I made a century that day which meant I could be included in the 1st team with immediate effect without anyone complaining. I'd been slightly concerned as never having played regular club cricket before was unsure as to what the standard would be, knowing that most of the team had minor county experience. Undoubtedly, it was a strong club and there was no shortage of comments about standards dropping by allowing 'fancy hatters' like me into the team! It was all in jest, of course, as most of them often played in 'fancy hat' teams when it suited but would not be seen dead in MCC or Free Foresters, let alone IZ, head wear. But nor would I, so I soon found myself very much part of the banter and camaraderie.

It was a real privilege to play on such a superb ground. Most of the college grounds were of very high quality indeed with full time groundsmen and the wherewithal to maintain standards, but the St John's ground was regarded understandably as one of the best. It was an excellent track and with a fast scoring outfield it led to some exciting cricket in an idyllic corner of north Oxford. Looking back at all the cricket I played, it was consistently the most enjoyable whilst at the same time of the highest club standard. The snag was we couldn't play 'at home' until term was over so May and June meant endless away fixtures unless we were drawn at home in a cup competition and we could manipulate to play on a day when the ground was free. If not, it was off to another ground, any ground, in Oxford.

League cricket was coming in with a vengeance at about this time and North Oxford had been invited to be part of the potentially very strong Thames Valley League, but because of this ground problem had had to refuse. Instead a new league was starting up locally called the Cherwell League which aimed to embrace all the better clubs in Oxfordshire. As three of these clubs used college grounds in Oxford the difficulty was understood and could be accommodated but it ruled out the customary arrangement of 1st and 2nd team fixtures each Saturday home and away against the same club. All this meant we tried to get fixtures against Thames Valley clubs on Sundays and our 2nd XI had to be content with irregular friendlies. It also partially explains why North Oxford had a thriving Thursday XI, an infamous local institution that was to prove to be a valuable source of practice, and amusement, for me some years later when increasing school and family commitments meant cricketing availability became curtailed. But for the time being I was very excited about being able to play regular cricket of a decent standard in what was clearly a more than competent side.

*

20/20 cricket is all the rage nowadays but it had its birth in club competitions many years ago. The Oxfordshire County Cricket Association, for example, organised its internal competition for all affiliated clubs on this basis. It gave the villages and smaller clubs the opportunity to pit their talents against the bigger clubs and their array of minor county players. The format certainly gave the lesser sides an opportunity and occasionally there were upsets but normally two of the powerful teams won through to the final. Extraordinarily this was played with the 40 over format which mitigated unfairly against the lesser teams whenever one of them reached that stage. The one occasion North Oxford met such a team in the final was spoilt by the imbalance of the sides, which would have been felt far less in a 20 over game.

Another advantage of the competition was that it gave a chance for any young or talented village cricketer to be noticed by the bigger brethren. One such moment occurred when we were drawn away to the idyllic village of Combe, with their tiny ground that doubled as a kind of village green. They were a presentable side who were rumoured to have a star player in a certain Roger Busby. He was tall, blonde with flowing locks, a modern day Adonis. He bowled fast, struck the ball miles and had a bullet-like throw. His efforts all but won the game for Combe, but we had just too many experienced players and of course he could only bowl five overs. The outcome though was that Alan Crossley, our wicket-keeper, deservedly at last now established as the county number one, explained to Roger that he was more than good enough to play for Oxfordshire but he was unlikely to be selected unless he played a higher standard of cricket on a regular basis. Why didn't he join North Oxford! Well, he did, with the result he had a long and successful career playing for the county and, of course, helped our club cause no end.

North Oxford v Headington, County Cup Final, 1975
Roger Busby seated far left, Trevor Gibson next to him,
Alan Crossley seated second from right

One of the better finals of those years that we were involved in was against Headington, a well-organised and popular club, with a sprinkling of county players. As usual it was played on the Christ Church ground, a very large and somewhat impersonal venue along the Iffley Road. It attracted a number of spectators and as usual the local press were out in force. We were strong favourites but were very wary of Headington's ability to play above themselves – they made a habit of upsetting the so-called top teams and, indeed, in the semi-final had knocked out the Jacks, or Cowley St John C.C., the only other Oxford side with a similar strength in depth to our own.

Richard Pineo won the toss and elected to field first. We had a strong bowling line-up with Roger Busby, John Stapleton, a seamer now past his best but still on his day a fine performer, Trevor Gibson, a left-arm spinner with a fiendish faster ball, and Graham Hobbins. The latter was 6'4" and could be decidedly quick and unpleasant. He'd played for Rhodesia's U19s but was too gentle and nice a chap to do his unbounded potential justice. They all bowled extremely well, the pick being John whose 10 overs cost just 12 runs and Trevor who got 3-33 off his 10. Headington couldn't cope with the relentless accuracy and but for a seventh wicket partnership of 43 which included some muscular hitting they would have been out of the game. As it was their 128 for nine off the allotted 40 overs looked barely adequate.

Alan Crossley was in good form, striking a sparkling 45 out of 64. The first wicket had fallen at 47 after 15 overs when I had joined him, but we saw the first sight of Headington's fighting qualities when Alan was brilliantly caught at deep square leg. Graham Hobbins and I then put on 50 before I was run out for 39 by a direct hit from Simon Porter the old Oxford Blue and stalwart of the county side. With four overs to go we were 118 for three. Eleven to win; seven wickets in hand; twenty-four balls. A doddle.

Graham and Martin Lloyd, our no. 5, scored four off the next over from Martin Lee, their opening seamer, before Graham was clean bowled. Simon Porter then conjured up a maiden over. 122 for four. Two overs remaining to get seven. Still a doddle.

Three accurate deliveries to Nigel Furley from Martin Lee produced no runs, and off the fourth ball, Nigel, trying to force it past mid-wicket was superbly caught by the fielder diving to his right. In comes Roger Busby with strict instructions to finish it off, but his middle stump is removed. Richard Pineo marches solidly to the wicket, plays the ball square on the off and sets off for a run. He is sent back by Martin Lloyd but before he can regain the crease, cover point hits the one stump he can see. 122 for seven. Three wickets in three balls. Now there is just one over to go with seven to win. Panic is rife.

In comes the old stalwart Trevor Gibson, no one better for a crisis, but Martin Lloyd is facing. He gets two off the second ball and a single off the fourth. The field is now closing in on Trevor, ready to pounce and keep him on strike. But cool as a cucumber, Trevor take a step down the wicket and cracks an imperious drive straight through the covers for the winning four. Phew!

*

Shotover is an idyllic country park just off Oxford's eastern by-pass. It can be spotted from afar by the radio/tv mast situated at the top of the hill. It is a lovely place to walk with stunning views from various points, south over towards the Berkshire Downs with Didcot Power Station conspicuous with its six cooling towers, or east over the Vale of Aylesbury with the lengthy escarpment of the Chilterns standing out in the distance. The woods give shelter from the rain or shade from the sun and with several well marked trails it is an ideal place to walk the dog or simply to wander peacefully around.

In 2008 on a beautiful summer's day I was with Bella our black labrador when we chanced upon a clearing amidst all the trees at the Horspath end. It was a beautiful, tranquil spot and someone had kindly put a bench, created from the trunk of an oak tree, in an ideal position to enjoy the vista. As I approached I saw it had a small brass plaque with an inscription. I put on my glasses ... and my heart stopped.

> In Loving Memory
> Trevor Anthony Gibson
> 1933 – 2005.

And above, a moving quotation:

> No stone stands over where he lies.
> It is in our hearts that his life is engraved.

I was stunned. Trevor lived in Horspath and spoke of his love of Shotover. It had to be him. I couldn't believe it. I sat down on the bench and all the memories came flooding back – of that lovely man, so kind, so friendly, always a good word for everyone, and what a cricketer ... so talented, yet so modest. I thought of all those games we'd played in as team mates and the many times he held the North Oxford bowling together, and, of course, that winning four in the Cup Final of some 30 years ago.

Happy days.

*

The North Oxford Thursday XI was something else. It had a regular fixture list, mostly against college sides early in the season and against villages later on. Although most of the side were club members there were invariably some ringers, undergraduates wanting a game or hauled in to make up the numbers and even players from other clubs in the same boat. Just occasionally a 1st team regular would turn out which had a dramatic impact on the strength of the side. They didn't win very often but normally put up a good enough show to make a decent game. Once my school and family commitments increased I had to stop playing regularly and fell back on the Thursday XI to keep my eye in with the occasional game. It was quite a revelation as I came across some remarkable characters, all in their own way in love with the game of cricket.

Paul Hayes, a history don at Keble, ran the side. He was a highly respected umpire in the local area and actually a very good one. He was rightly in demand to officiate non-first-class matches in The Parks, important league games and national club knock-out ones. But on a Thursday he played, and he certainly made his presence felt. It was extraordinary that in changing his white coat for his whites his whole persona seemed to change as well.

He was a nice enough chap but he did possess a fierce temper which was all too frequently unleashed on any person, especially the young, whom he felt had let his side down. The trouble was he wasn't a good enough cricketer to do as well as he wanted himself so he vented his frustrations on those under him. Of course Paul fancied himself as a batsman, bowler and captain so there was plenty of scope for things to go wrong. He was also very tense and I suspect suffered from high blood pressure – in fact a human time-bomb just waiting to go off. There was always a certain tension each Thursday as we awaited the first incident!

If you were unlucky it would happen before the start. You just needed to turn up late and both barrels would be unloaded on you. Undergraduates are not the greatest time-keepers and several rather good players appeared just the once, late, scored a fifty and were never seen again understandably not prepared to take the verbal bashing a second time. Of course, you could drop a catch, especially off Paul's bowling and the rest of us would cringe as we awaited the choice verbals that inevitably followed. And being well versed in the English language his vocabulary was extensive. Run outs, too, would lead to interesting exchanges especially if it involved him … and, needless to say, he was never at fault. He took each and every game so seriously you just had to laugh at it all. I was spared his worst venom as he was keen that I played whenever I could, but I did drop a catch off him once. He was about to explode, then just in time remembered who it was and satisfied himself with: "Huh ... I can see why you don't play for the 1st team any more." Thank you, Paul.

A total contrast to Paul was the previous captain and team manager, Eric Neale, who sadly had stopped running the side before I appeared, but he still played regularly and was a wise enough old bird to ignore Paul's antics. Eric was the salt of the earth, as genuine and as pleasant a person as you could wish to meet. He was up at dawn each day to organize his milk distribution rotas as I knew all too well through popping over the road in Summertown to buy a paper first thing and seeing him in action. Eric would joke and say it was all right for these lazy teachers to get up at seven, the people who mattered had already done a day's work. And in the dark and teeming rain of mid-winter he'd still be there with a smile on his face and a friendly word.

He really enjoyed his cricket. He bowled a bit, batted at seven or eight and always played his part in a small way, often holding on at the crease to enable a draw, as he was difficult to get out. He liked the company and the camaradie of a team game and afterwards would always stay for a pint, rarely any more, before loyally returning to his wife and the necessary early night. Anno domini caused him to struggle a bit in the field and he was always grateful if someone did the chasing for him. I once asked him what it was that kept him playing so enthusiastically. He quickly replied: "I love it, Nigel, I really love it. And once I stop I shall never be able to start again. While I feel I can still contribute in a small way I'll carry on as long as I can." Eric certainly contributed. It was people like him that made playing the game so pleasurable.

Another character was Tony Lurcock, again an academic. He had no pretensions about his ability and was actually a more effective a player then he would have you believe. The 1st team was not his scene although he did play on odd occasions; he was a genuine 2nd XI man, indeed he skippered the side for a year or two if I remember rightly. But on Thursdays he was in his element as one of the better players and a genuine all-rounder. His was a shapely, rotund figure whose run-up was more of a waddle, but his military medium was effective as it was generally on a length and occasionally he hit the seam. His batting was effective, too, as a middle order man who would hit out or defend according to the need. He was a real team player.

Tony was a very popular member of the side as he was a totally genuine person who enjoyed the social life of a cricket club as much as the game itself. He involved himself in club matters by serving on the committee and put himself out to welcome newcomers. He was the ideal person to enjoy a drink with as he was interested in everything and everyone least of all himself. He had an excellent sense of humour which he frequently used to effect against himself. Once I ran him out in a run chase and he waved aside all attempts at an apology. "My figure has seen better days and I'm no longer as sylph-like as I think I am. I need moments like that to remind me … after all, I could have sent you back." He was a valued friend in those days, and I suspect most of the club would have said the same of him.

Ian MacFarlane was another wise old bird. He was one of the elder brethren who'd seen it all before and Paul's histrionics was just water off a duck's back to Ian. He bowled a very good line of orthodox left-arm in which his flight and guile got him as many wickets as the actual spin. And he had a wicked sense of humour always seeing the funny side of even the most dire of situations. He'd flick the lengthy strands of grey hair out of his eyes, grin from ear to ear and pronounce judgement. Woe betide any team mate or opponent who had airs or graces or pretensions above his station. Ian was an academic, too, inevitably in Oxford, and a game of cricket was the highlight of his week. He'd often get more than one game as his bowling skills were not out of place at a higher level, but he found the fielding a strain, all too understandably. As with others of his ilk he was excellent company over a pint, keen to analyse his and the team's performance without ever taking the game too seriously. He was a great supporter of the young, happy to put up with the trends of the age and always seeing the positive side of any character. I think it helped keep him youthful in outlook but his bowling merited their respect anyway, so it was not difficult for them to relate to him. I have fond memories of cricket in Ian's company too.

Such were some of the Thursday XI characters – all ordinary people, not especially gifted players, but with a common love for the game of cricket. It doesn't matter at what level you play, or what the result is, your team mates can often determine whether a day's cricket is worthwhile or not. At North Oxford, in whichever side, I was very lucky indeed.

9. OXFORDSHIRE

One of the implications of joining North Oxford was that I became eligible to play for the county side. My registration was still with Essex and Lou Frewer, the Oxfordshire secretary asked at an early stage if I'd be happy for him to approach them in order to transfer it. Essex, not surprisingly, had no objections and before I knew what was happening I had been asked to play in Oxfordshire's first game of the season, a one day trial game in The Parks against the University early in June.

The University were not a strong side by first-class standards but at near full strength they were expected to be more than a match for a half strength minor county XI, that contained two or three newcomers like myself, several experienced campaigners and the balance made up of local players whose club form had earned them a chance. Additionally we were to be skippered for the first time by Peter Smith who had recently been appointed to the captaincy.

Peter won the toss and elected to bat, but at 27 for three we were soon in trouble and I was at the crease quicker than anticipated. It was an idyllic ground to play cricket, a large open expanse but surrounded by a glorious array of trees bedecked in their colourful blossom, with the distinguished looking pavilion incongruously sitting in the midst of this magnificent parkland. The track was slow and the outfield damp after overnight rain but the University bowlers kept a tight line and gave little away. I was joined in the middle by Robin Winstone, a colleague from North Oxford, and riding our luck we put on 52 in even time. I was dropped twice on my way to 54 which turned out to be the highest score of the day, and Robin patiently eked out 23 the equal second highest. It was a battle all the way and it took us three hours and nearly 65 overs to reach 141 for eight before Peter declared giving the University 25 minutes less to get the runs.

Surprisingly the Dark Blues were never in the hunt and were bowled out for a paltry 64 in 43 overs. The damage was chiefly done by our skipper who returned 3-11 off 10 overs with his fast-medium cutters, and Simon Porter whose off-spin returned 2-9 off 9 overs. I contributed one of my better catches, diving to my left at short square to grab a sharp bat/pad chance, tactfully off our captain's bowling. But it was pleasing to run out such easy winners even if it was no surprise when the joint University side to play the tourists two days later had a 'controversial' eight/three split in favour of Cambridge. From my own point of view I had probably done well enough to merit selection for the minor county championship matches which were due to start in July.

*

I played for Oxfordshire on and off for four years and although I never really established myself in the team there were plenty of high points and amusing moments to have made the experience well worthwhile. It was two day cricket in the seventies which is a fiendishly hard game to play properly with two competent sides on a decent wicket. It is almost impossible to get a result unless the captains show some imagination with declarations and target setting. Luckily in Peter Smith we had just the right man as quite apart from his considerable ability with both ball and bat, he had the intelligence to know the best way to go about winning a match. He realised the important cricket was played on day two and so on occasions sacrificing a first innings lead, and the associated points, could reap dividends later in the game. He wasn't a manipulator, he just cleverly played the system to try and get the best chance of winning a game for his own side. In so doing Oxfordshire occasionally lost a game, but more often they won one. He was an inspirational captain and quite the best I ever played under. It was no surprise he turned Oxfordshire's fortunes around. In his first season we qualified for inclusion in the Gillette Cup and in 1974 he achieved the ultimate accolade of winning the minor county championship. He resolutely refused to follow the policy of most other counties of signing ex-first-class players, insisting that we should remain true to our roots by selecting just from those playing for clubs in the county. Inevitably this led to a tremendous team spirit and although the core of the side was built up of younger newcomers brought in by Peter, he was never afraid to turn to older, more experienced players if and when the occasion demanded. Above all, he built a team, the sum of whose parts were far greater than just the abilities of the individual players. People wanted to play for him because it was fun, he was very fair with each individual and we all knew the team was going places. The 1974 triumph took quite a few people by surprise. It was only the second time Oxfordshire had won the title (the first being as long ago as 1928) and there were no big names in the side. It was undoubtedly true that each individual played above himself, but the key was the captain. Peter Smith won that championship though his inspirational leadership.

Sadly, I only played twice that season. I just couldn't get into the side, so well was everyone playing. I batted quite well in those two games but, maddeningly, it counted for very little in the end as both were rain affected and no result was possible. In the first, at St Edward's School in Oxford I scored 64 not out to help win the three points for a first innings' lead; and in the second at Henley it was a speedy 31 in a vain attempt to beat the clock in a run chase. My performances, although pleasing, rightly did not justify displacing the first choice batsmen when they were available.

There were two sequels to that memorable season which epitomised the way Peter Smith ran his side. At a celebratory dinner the following winter, from which sadly I had to cry off at the last minute due to sickness, all the players were presented with an engraved tankard to commemorate winning the championship. Only thirteen people represented the county that year and numbers twelve and thirteen played just twice each. But we still both received a tankard. And secondly, Peter determined that the XI to represent the county in the first round of next season's Gillette Cup would be selected from those thirteen. He was true to his word despite the unnecessary criticism he received from the local press as I was

Peter Smith

called into the team when a batsman was injured. So I played against Cornwall and my unremarkable score of nine is therefore qualified to be recorded in Cricinfo's archive of English players for the whole world to see how useless I was! The ticket, required for entry into the Morris Motors ground for the match, shows that supporters were charged the princely sum of 60p to come and watch me play! But Peter's gesture of rewarding my remaining available throughout his triumphant season was hugely appreciated. My time was up and I knew it would be my last game, but we won and it was as good an occasion as any to finish on.

*

So where had it all gone wrong for me to play just twenty-four games over four years? I didn't score enough runs, it was as simple as that. It went wrong from day one, barely a month after that encouraging debut in The Parks. The first championship game was played at Swindon away to Wiltshire. It was a depressing ground to play on with one side of the field a huge concrete wall, the back of a Swindon Town F.C. stand. The pavilion was a large impersonal building with tiered seating above the dressing-rooms and clubhouse, so that watching the game you were quite high up. And I watched a lot! Asked to bat at number 3, I was padded up, and, inevitably, raring to go. Then the opening pair of Mike Nurton and Stan Hahn put on over 180 and weren't parted until after 3.30pm. It was a stifling hot day and by the time I got to the crease I was exhausted just watching and concentrating. It was no surprise that I was out second ball for a duck. Two years later this fixture was on the same ground and batting second I was lower in the order and not out for not very many overnight. The next morning we were going to bat for the two remaining overs that determined the first innings lead and the relevant three points. We required 12 runs to achieve this and my partner and I agreed that if at all possible we'd try to ease the pressure with a single, or more, off the first ball. I was the non-striker and shot off as the delivery was driven smartly into the covers. The ball went straight to a fielder who instantly threw down the stumps at the bowler's end with me stranded! There was no run, and no call, and I'd failed again. Swindon was certainly not one of my favourite grounds.

Even if I did little of note whilst playing for Oxfordshire, there was an occasion when it is just possible to argue, certainly by myself, that one shot led to a victory. It was against Dorset on, thanks to the weather, a pretty poor pitch at Poole Park in 1971. Dorset had employed the services of the famous Derek Shackleton and this was a wicket on which he was likely to run through a side. We played poorly on the first day and struggled to compete in the first innings. Peter Smith, at his inspirational best, cut his losses and declared our first innings closed 25 runs behind, thereby surrendering the three points and gambling on a sporting reply from his opposite number. This duly came when we were asked to score 159 in two hours, but against the mighty Shack. He hadn't got many wickets in the first innings, but equally we had hardly scored any runs off him. If he shut up one end we had no chance. It was determined Mike Nurton would act as an anchor and keep the score ticking over whilst the rest of us would give it a go from the other end while we were in with a chance. I went in at number three after half an hour when the score was 27, but Shack was conceding very few. My first two balls from him were typical. Just short of a length, moving slightly off the seam and all you could do was pat them back. I spoke to Mike and said this would get us nowhere, I was going to give him the charge. Mike said well, watch it as he'll drop it short or bowl it quicker and wider. Wise words! The next ball I faced, I took two steps down the wicket and expected the shorter delivery which arrived on cue. I kept my head down, waited a fraction, kept my eye fixed on the ball and swung through the line with all my might. I struck the ball right in the meat of the bat and it soared high over the deep mid on boundary and out of the Park! There were gasps from the fielders, even I was surprised, and wild cheers from the pavilion but the best part was that Shack looked shocked as it took some time to retrieve the ball. The next delivery I advanced again and this time it was the quicker one down the leg-side which I swept over mid-wicket one bounce for four. I contented myself with that until his next over, the first ball of which I carved over cow corner for four. But then the maestro won the battle as I failed to get to the pitch of one and holed out at deep long off. The cameo was worth only 14 runs but it won a psychological battle. He could be hit and the remaining batsmen all contributed speedily and we won by four wickets and ten balls to spare. Shack was the most expensive bowler, conceding 76. This victory guaranteed our position in the top five of the minor counties table and therefore qualification for the following season's Gillette Cup.

Oxfordshire left-hander Nigel Chapman plays a straight bat to a ball from Shackleton during the Minor Counties match with Dorset at St Edwards School yesterday.

*

This Oxfordshire side of the early seventies was a blend of good local club players with no stars or egos to cater for. A few were notable for their exceptional performances like Brian Jeffries, an all-rounder from Banbury, whose live-wire character, nifty seamers and powerful hitting in the middle order frequently made a difference; Alan Crossley, an outstanding wicket-keeper/opening batsman from North Oxford, who had been ignored for selection before Peter's arrival and now rightly cemented his place for many years to come; Giles Ridley, an Oxford Blue whose left-arm spin and lower order batting provided a touch of class. And Simon Porter, another Oxford Blue, an accurate off-spinner and useful lower order bat, a very loyal Headington C.C. man who later served county and University in positions of prominence. Then there was Phil Garner, from Cowley St John, who struggled like myself to score runs in these years, but he battled through to become one of the county's most successful and longest serving captains earning himself in due course a place in the XI of the Century. But there were two who stood out. One, Peter Smith, whose outstanding captaincy I've already described, was equally capable of winning a match with either his bowling or his batting. The other became a minor county legend.

Mike Nurton first played for Oxfordshire in 1963, aged 20 and finally retired after the 1990 season. In that time he scored 12,713 runs which was an all-time minor counties record. He won a Benson & Hedges Gold Award, the only minor counties player ever to do so, v Lancashire in 1978, and was selected in the minor counties team of the century. The statistics are mightily impressive but they pale into insignificance when you consider the character of the man. He was so modest and unassuming that it was easy to regard him as ordinary. He was a left-hander like myself and although he would never presume to advise he was always willing to help whenever asked, as I did frequently. There was one particular bowler from Devon, Doug Yeabsley, whom I couldn't cope with at all. He bowled left-arm over at a quick pace and could move the ball either way off the seam. Even Mike rated him and reckoned he could have held his own in the first-class game had he been so inclined. I was easy meat and he'd have me caught in the slips or bowled in next to no time. So I asked Mike how he coped. 'With difficulty,' was his immediate response such was the respect he had, 'but I find it helps if I can get across the off stump, then I have three options depending on the line and length – play him through the covers, through mid-wicket, or leave it. If I'm in the right place I shouldn't be lbw or bowled.' Ever looking to complicate the issue, I then asked 'but how do you know which way the ball's going to move?' 'I don't,' he smiled. And that, I suppose, was his secret. He had a method, kept it simple and if it didn't come off he didn't fret about it, as next time it probably would. He was a lovely, friendly character whose value I didn't fully appreciate until some ten years or so after he'd retired.

I hadn't seen him for about 25 years when I belatedly discovered he was a magician, a member of the Magic Circle no less. I knew he was Head of PE and coaching sport at Sherborne School so I phoned him and asked if he'd come and do a magic show for the boys at Horris Hill. He'd be delighted, he said, and we had a wonderful evening. The show was fabulous, to the extent that the boys demanded he be asked back again. I unearthed from him that he'd become a Lay Preacher, so two years later he agreed to come and give another show on the Saturday evening, stay the night and preach in Chapel on the Sunday morning. And on both occasions he was outstanding, especially getting the level right for prep school boys in the Service, an art that very few preachers achieve. We had a lovely time on the Saturday evening, chatting about cricket, mutual friends, our teaching careers and, above all, Oxfordshire. I was astonished he could remember details of games I'd played in when you think I was involved for merely four of his twenty-seven seasons. And not once was there any mention of his remarkable achievements. He is a remarkably unassuming man and yet so wonderfully talented. It was a real joy to have had the chance to meet up again so fruitfully all those years later. All made possible through the game of cricket.

10. RURAL JOYS

It was that wretched phone. Any thoughts of a decent lie in disappeared with the persistent ringing. First day of the eagerly anticipated summer holidays and it was barely 8 o'clock. And that phone was clearly not going to stop.

'It's bound to be John,' mumbled my wife, Lindsay, from deep under the duvet. 'You go.'

Bleary-eyed and half-asleep, I stumbled into the hallway and picked up the receiver.

'Ah, good, you're down then,' said the all too recognisable voice, as keen as ever.

'Yes, John. Late last night.'

'Are the boys with you? ... I'm three short for this afternoon ... and what about the Lanes? ... are they here yet?'

'Yes and I don't know,' I replied as completely as possible.

'Can I count on Ben and Tom?,' he said quickly, then only slightly more sheepishly, 'and you wouldn't like a game yourself by any chance, would you?'

'Where and when, John?'

'2.15. Loxhore. Lovely ground. And you can tell Tom the best teas in Devon.'

That swung it. 'OK, John, count on all three of us. But where's Loxhore?'

'Easy,' he said, 'just take the Bratton Fleming road out of Barnstaple, then turn off left when you see a sign to Loxhore. Can't miss it. Very good of you. See you this afternoon.' And with that he put down the phone and left me gaping, wondering what I'd let ourselves in for.

John Edwards kept North Devon C.C. going. Secretary, team manager, captain of the midweek XI and general dogsbody, there was nothing he wouldn't do for the game of cricket. Still playing at 70+ his medium-to-slow, slow bowling commanded respect if only to save face in the bar afterwards as no-one wanted the ridicule for getting out to him. He was the ideal captain, making sure everyone got involved no matter how young – and he needed the schoolboys to make up his teams. Ben and Tom were 12 and 11 and there were certain to be two or three others playing today. But his geography was notoriously weak so I soon got out the road atlas. Yes, there was Bratton Fleming ... but there were three variations of Loxhore.

It was as well we started out earlier than usual. Devon lanes are well known for their hedges, you simply can't see over them. Turning left at the sign for Loxhore was easy enough ... but that was it. No further signs, just a maze of bends, forks, crossroads and the occasional farmhouse, none of which were visible until they were upon you. No semblance of a village, let alone a cricket club. It was a lovely summer's day outside the car and the temperature was rising inexorably inside it.

"Dad, are we going the right way ... there's grass growing in the middle of the road?"

"Dad, the game starts soon."

"Oh, look, Dad, there's a cricket field!"

And, miraculously, there through the trees was a greensward with a very obvious square in the middle, and a building appearing to the side that had every look of a pavilion. We soon came to some houses and a gateway that clearly led to the ground. Triumph!

"There we are, boys, no trouble at all!"

"Not many people here, yet," said Ben, a bit too observantly for my liking.

We got our kit out of the boot, and walked round the side of the pavilion ... to be greeted by the sign 'Bratton Fleming C.C.', and very little else. No-one to be seen.

Oh.

We hurried back to the car, flung the kit in and set off again.

"We'll have to ask someone where Loxhore is," I said, trying to regain control over a rapidly deteriorating situation.

"Yes, Dad, but who?"

A not unreasonable question as we hadn't actually seen anyone at all for about twenty minutes.

"Um ... the first person we see. Keep your eyes out."

Fortuitously, as we turned down yet another lane, there was a lady walking along the road carrying a large bag. We drew up beside her and put the window down.

"Excuse me," said Ben, keen to assume control, "but can you tell us where the Loxhore cricket ground is?"

"Of course, dear, in fact I'm on my way there now as I'm helping with the tea. It's just down the hill here and then left."

Not to miss this golden chance, Ben quickly vacated his seat and ushered the old dear in to the front. "It's quite easy really," she said, "once you know."

It was downhill, and it was to the left, but through a farm gate and the cricket field was still hidden by another hedge. No houses in sight, just a remarkably new looking, small single story building that served as the pavilion, well protected by hedges and trees. Thanks, John. Can't miss it! ... not once you know.

It was 2.20 and we were not the last to arrive. Luckily John had won the toss and tactfully elected to bat seeing he was still five short at the time.

"Ah, Ben, good. I want you to open the batting, so be quick as they want to get started. And Tom, I'm playing you as a bowler today so you're 10. And Nigel, you wouldn't do the first stint of umpiring, would you?" Within seconds of arrival, good old John had us all sorted and dispatched.

There were several familiar midweek XI faces. Roger Rushton, opening bat and keeper, the lovely rotund and ruby faced Henry Pearson, a vicar on his annual holiday away from his Wiltshire parish, ex-policeman Howard Clifton, well known for a short fuse and saying what he thought but a very useful all-rounder, and Charlie Foulkes who could hold his own better in the bar than on the field of play. In addition to Ben and Tom there were two other lads playing, one of whom, Robert Gear, I recalled looking particularly promising the year before.

It was an idyllic setting. Rolling hills all around, barely a building in sight, just farm fields intermingled with copses and hedgerows. And the sun shone down on a perfect English summer's afternoon. Umpiring was a delight, even if concentration was not easy, in such a setting. The field though was an unusual shape – very long and narrow. Boundaries square of the wicket were a near impossibility, whereas it was no distance to the hedges behind the bowler. I mused that it would have been fun to have had John Price, the old Middlesex and England fast bowler, coming in off his lengthy run here – he'd have had to have begun it a field or two away!

The North Devon innings proceeded without, unusually, any major upset. Roger got his usual 30 odd; Ben contributed a sensible 20; the padre sparkled to an impressive and speedy 50, wisely utilising the straight boundaries to spare himself any unnecessary running; Robert produced a more sedate but equally impressive 50; the other lads added their bit and it was all rounded off by the constabulary smiting 33 in twelve balls. Regardless of the score, John always declared at tea but on this occasion with 209 for seven on the board he was able to do so some five minutes early, doubtless to enable everyone to do justice to the meal we had been anticipating.

If John had been vague with the directions, he was spot on about the tea. What a feast! The two trestle-tables were groaning under the spread put before us – scones with clotted cream and home-made strawberry jam, Scotch pancakes liberally spread with farm butter, salad rolls, sausage rolls, sandwiches of every description, shortbread, fruit cake, coffee cake, jam sponge cake, chocolate roulade, and I suppose with the kids in mind, jelly and ice-cream to round it off. Tom, not being required to bat, had taken advantage and was already tucking into a well loaded plate by the time the rest of us appeared, clearly intent on second helpings. The mobility of N. Devon C.C. midweek XI in the field, not its strongest point at the best of times, was going to be severely compromised. The Rev. Henry, a gourmet of some note, was intent on doing justice too. Clearly, John's decision on who was to field first slip, would require some care. The Ladies of Loxhore had done everyone proud and it was with no little reluctance, half an hour or so later, that the N. Devon team took to the field.

If the fielding positions were simple – the youngsters either side of the wicket square, aged gentlemen straight and on the boundary – the bowling decisions were not. John, of course, opened but three of his first over were deposited nonchalantly over the hedge behind him. Howard bowled the second over and received similar treatment. Immediately he pontificated to John as to how could he possibly be expected to bowl against the wind, up the slope and into the sun, he just did not know. John mildly pointed out there was barely a zephyr, the field was remarkably flat for rural Devon and the sun was behind the clouds. He suggested he took a rest and waited for the other end to be freed. John's second over was not much better and at 47 for nought after three overs, the 209 was looking horribly insignificant. At which point he turned to Tom.

"Just the one over for now, Tom, so we can change ends."

Tom's first ball was a slow parabola, with a little tweak of off-spin. Judging from his expression and even bigger backlift, the local Loxhore farmer clearly felt such trivia should be dispatched two fields into the distance. Sadly (for him) but inevitably, the bat came down far too soon and the resulting top edge sent the ball high into the sky with early calculations suggesting a likely landing area not far behind Tom. Sensible lad, he'd done his bit and was clearly intent on staying clear of the ensuing action. And well he might, as approaching rapidly, (well, as rapidly as possible) from the mid off boundary was the not to be messed with figure of The Law; while at the same time, if not quite so rapidly, there approached from the mid on boundary the not inconsiderable figure, enhanced by that splendid tea, of The Church. Sadly, in the light of ensuing events, the ball was erring towards the on rather than the off, so it was with no little conviction, and with the backing, presumably, of the Almighty that the good padre called "Mine ... Mine." The Law, was, however, especially in the light of his humiliation the previous over, not going to be denied a moment of glory and with eyes fixed on the ball, hands at the ready, was inexorably moving into ecclesiastical territory, shouting for all his worth "I've got it ... I've got it." Unless the captain exerted authority there was going to be the Mother of all collisions. Poor John, though, was in a terrible quandary. A regular Church goer he knew all too well that with God's help the ball would be caught and God would certainly be on Henry's side; yet not once in his life had he opposed the Law and after his recent exchange this was not a good moment to reject Howard, so he did the only thing he possibly could in the circumstances, and that was to say nothing.

Meanwhile the ball was approaching terra firma at an alarming speed and remarkably arrived into the good Vicar's outstretched hands at the very moment that Howard careered into him sending them both sprawling on the ground with yelps of both joy and agony. The joy was that of his holiness who, clearly used to keeping his hands together, had somehow clung onto the ball; the agony from our ex-policeman who wildly kicking one leg in the air like some epileptic bronco, was screeching to all and sundry that he was critically injured and couldn't possibly bowl again. But we, and Tom, had a wicket!

The batsmen, amidst all this excitement, had changed ends, so Tom's second ball, after a discreet delay, was directed not to the new batsman, one of their youngsters, but to the other big hitting opener. You'd have thought he'd have learnt from his partner's indiscretion that Tom merited at least a modicum of respect, but, no, he charged down the wicket, misjudged the flight completely and was easily stumped by Roger. The rest of the over was treated with the utmost care. 47 for two.

John's bowling now came into its own as the callow youth at no. 3 had no idea how to cope with these gentle lobs that were dead straight and bang on a length. After two overs of patting them back he took a wild swing and was bowled. Tom, of course, was allowed to continue and from its frenzied beginning the innings descended into a more sedate affair with just the occasional boundary and the odd single here and there.

Despite, as usual, being desperately short of bowling, John sensibly did not prevail upon Howard, realising all too well the short shrift he would get. Tom had been replaced by Robert, who being both older and taller, bowled his spinners a bit flatter and quicker and had picked up a couple of wickets. At 105 for five the game was well balanced when the Loxhore captain came to the crease. Dave Amos was a lovely man, played the game for fun and always made sure everyone in his team got involved. The life and soul of Loxhore as John was of North Devon. But Dave was no mean batsman and on merit should have been in at no. 3. He set about controlling the run chase with consumate skill, playing each ball on its merits and not taking the semblance of a risk. The score mounted and the bowlers tired. Seeing the moment required heroic intervention, Howard approached John.

"I think I could give it a go again, John, if you wanted."

"Oh, Howard. Are you sure? That would be very good of you. I quite thought you wouldn't be able to manage it. What about trying the other end next over?"

Superbly handled, John!

Dave played Howard's first ball through mid-wicket for one, but then the obdurate no. 4 was castled by a beauty. Pitching outside off, it cut viciously in to hit middle and leg. 187 for six. Two youngsters were removed reasonably quickly and at 198 for eight things were getting tense. But Dave was too good and with three classic boundaries, all along the ground, he took Loxhore home.

All was not over, though, as back in the pavilion the remains of tea had been left out to be finished! Tom managed another plateful before a contented family trio wended their way through the Devon lanes back home.

*

The picturesque High Bickington cricket field was spoilt by a concrete edifice more suited to minor rural football grounds, but it served as a sort of pavilion and provided some cover from the elements for any spectators. Not that there were many on the day of North Devon 3rd XI's visit and indeed the weather was glorious. John's team raising had been less fraught than normal and I was spared the embarrassment of having either to perform or umpire and so settled down at the boundary edge to watch the game unfold and hope Ben and Tom would uphold the family name.

High Bickington won the toss and chose to bat on a pretty good wicket for a village square. John as usual kept one end going but the locals were wise to his ways and means and were certainly not going to be tempted into any indiscretions. There was no obvious bowler to open the other end so everyone who could turn an arm was given a chance. Various deliveries were removed in good agricultural fashion into the neighbouring fields but at the same time wickets fell at regular intervals. Tom managed a respectable spell of 2-29 off seven overs and even Ben had someone caught on the boundary. The Bickington innings had taken its allotted time when the tenth wicket fell on 158. A respectable score, but an eminently gettable one.

Tea did not delay the participants quite so long on this occasion, and Tom's disappointment here was probably reflected in his early dismissal for a duck. As usual, Roger Rushton kept the early part of the innings going with a sound 39 and but for the good Padre being unnecessarily run out for a fluent 24 progress towards our target would have been relatively comfortable. As it was Henry's dismissal led to a flurry of wickets, and the score was just 128 when the ninth wicket fell and the good John was called upon to make one of his very rare appearances with the bat. He joined Ben who at 18 not out had managed to retain his wicket amidst the sudden carnage.

They made a fine pair. Ben aged 12, keen, sprightly and quick to spot a run; John aged 72, slightly doddery, bespectacled and agonizingly slow. John immediately took charge. "I'll keep my end up. You get the runs. But NO quick singles." And he was as good as his word. The one shot John could play was the forward defence, with an immaculately straight bat, and this was churned out ball after ball. Ben in the meantime was equally watchful but every so often unleashed an attacking shot of some venom which raced to the boundary.

High Bickington were by now getting somewhat frustrated and even went to the length of conceding a very long single just to get the batsmen to change ends. But it made no difference. The continued defiance and precocious strokeplay meant that we reached the final over of the day on 154 for nine. But John, on 2 not out, was facing, and there was no way he was going to get the necessary 5 runs. Somehow they were going to have to change ends.

The field closed in to cut off any chance of a single. Ben backed up excessively, to the extent he received a polite warning from the bowler, but four balls had been bowled and the score was unchanged. John called a Summit Meeting in the middle of the wicket to discuss the urgency of action. It was agreed that come what may, they would run the next ball in a valiant attempt to win the match.

It was at this moment that all his years of cricketing experience came to John's rescue. He realised he had to play a different shot. What, he was not sure, but some years earlier he had been known to dab one past gully, and earlier still he had had mild success with a sort of scoop to leg. On this occasion it was the latter that was brought into action. The ball was slightly directed to the legside and, with a quick prayer, out came the scoop. Luckily he made contact, otherwise it would have been plumb LBW. But it was a top edge which lobbed terrifying close to the swooping leg gully who valiantly, but mistakenly, dived to catch it. He couldn't quite reach it and in the attempt missed the ball which progressed a yard or two behind him. In the meantime Ben had already made his ground at the receiver's end and John had made three steps' progress in his marathon towards the other. Inevitably everyone was shouting at the prone fielder, a large, rotund Devon publican who was quite incapable of a rapid return to the vertical. The wicket-keeper at last realizing this, flung off his gloves and sped towards the ball. John by now was more than halfway towards the bowler's end, and dare one say it, gathering momentum. On reaching the ball, the gallant custodian plucked it from the ground and flung it with all his might at the further wicket. A second later, dear John received this missile right on his backside, and the poor man collapsed in a heap on the pitch. But with bat outstretched, he had made his ground!

With the one ball remaining, Ben danced down the wicket and whacked it first bounce into the hedge. North Devon 3rd XI had achieved a remarkable victory. Ben grinned from ear to ear. John hobbled from the scene vigorously massaging his rear. And the following week the local Journal had the appropriate headline amidst its sports section 'Young and Old Stage Super Win.'

*

John Edwards

It had been a good tour. Unusually, there had been four full days of cricket and, thankfully, a victory had been achieved on the Monday. Nimmers had fallen out of the hotel window one night (and all tourists had been sworn to secrecy lest his Mum heard about it); Nicko, thankfully, had kept his President's speech at the North Devon dinner on the Monday to a bare minimum; Scotty had been caught on camera on the Link Road at a mere 105 mph on the return journey from Sidmouth; Jabba had been totally wasted on just two evenings and he and Barn had to spend the Thursday night in the pavilion at Instow, neither being capable of returning (or being returned) to the hotel. The hotel manager had seen enough of them to make it clear that he would not welcome them back the following year. Oh, and Coxy had fallen over and cut his chin during Wednesday evening's barbeque. So as Saracens tours go it had been pretty successful and relatively incident free: P4 W1 D1 L2 compared favourably to a lot of years and with the Bridgetown game to conclude the week there was a chance, just a chance, of a second victory.

A win on the Monday is crucial. Few of the side are hung over, most are raring to get started, and some are moderately fit. Things inevitably peak. Tuesday is a somewhat harder affair after a heavy and late night. Wednesday and Thursday are simply impossible unless reinforcements are coming. Friday, though, against a village side, with an afternoon start, always offers a chance of success.

Bridgetown has one of the most attractive grounds in the country, indeed a plaque hangs proudly in the pavilion to commemorate winning an award to that effect. Nestled at the eastern end of Exmoor, the setting slopes steeply down to the floodplain of the River Exe and the river itself borders the ground and acts as a barrier to the main road that would otherwise be a bit too close for comfort. One can sit contentedly outside the pavilion at the top of the ground, basking in the sunshine, looking down on the action below you while at the same time soaking in the stunning scenery.

Ben was overall tour manager but as usual had lost any semblance of control by about 10.35pm on the Monday night. Sensibly, therefore, the captaincy had been shared out and each day this delicate decision was made at breakfast dependent on the state of health of the various contenders. It's a good system but eyebrows were raised on this particular Friday when it was announced that Dave would lead the troops at Bridgetown. Big Dave is a lovely chap, the perfect tourist – bachelor,

Bridgetown, Somerset

gets on with everyone, wonderful sense of humour, solid drinker. But his greatest asset is that he keeps wicket. He'd be the first to admit his keeping is not perfect (although it does seem to improve in the bar after several pints), but he performs that vital role when no-one else can. His batting is better not mentioned but the concern on this occasion was that he immediately announced that having been invested with the captaincy he was not going to keep wicket as he intended to bowl. He had a very good line in leg-spin, he said, and had been listening to Richie Benaud so had developed not just a googly but a flipper too. He planned to unleash these weapons on the unsuspecting locals of Bridgetown. Luckily half the team were still in bed so didn't hear this staggering announcement; the few that did, were so taken aback and hung over they were lost for words, and somnolently returned to their Full English and appropriate pages of The Sun.

A minor problem with a fixture at Bridgetown is actually getting there from the tour base in Bideford. It's not the finding of it that's tricky, but Friday is the final day of the tour which means packing up and loading all personal paraphernalia and more pertinently not getting caught too long for lunch in one of the many tempting hostelries en route. The Royal Oak at either Withypool or Washford are especially dangerous as they are enticingly close to Bridgetown and well known for their excellent fare. In fact as Dave tossed up he was still four short but was not unduly worried as there seemed to be an unwritten agreement that

Bridgetown always fielded first, and Tom and Jabba were already present as they liked to open and knew only too well that if they were late they'd be 10 and Jack. They'd cunningly lunched in The Badgers Holt Inn on the main road a mere fifty yards from the ground so could time their arrival to perfection.

So the two largest (by some way) members of the touring party strode out to the middle together to get proceedings underway. The great thing about this opening pair was that supporters knew there would be some good entertainment. The partnership might not last long but the scoring rate would be fast. They eschewed running whenever possible, preferring instead to deal in boundaries especially of the aerial variety. Such was the case on this occasion as the Bridgetown openers, admittedly military medium, were regularly dispatched into neighbouring fields. There was a delay of some eight minutes after a particularly fine pull from Jabba landed in the middle of the River Exe and the ball was carried rapidly downstream before some local youths were able to pluck it out with the fishing net provided for just that purpose. The score was 112 when Tom holed out at deep long off for an excellent 60 and Jabba followed shortly afterwards when the ignorant no. 3 called him for a short single and he was all too easily run out. Progress thereafter was less dramatic but somewhat safer, and Big Dave was able to declare just before half time on a pleasing 229 for five, knowing that was almost certainly beyond the reach of the home team. In fact in all the previous encounters their highest total had been 170.

By now the selected XI were all present and correct but were somewhat apprehensive while tea was being enjoyed as the captain had yet to decree who was to be invested with the pads and gloves of the office that was traditionally his. Word had spread about his intentions which initially had caused amusement, but now, as the moment approached were beginning to cause alarm. The wicket-keeping choice was no problem for Dave. He was a schoolmaster, a Deputy Headmaster no less; this was an Old Boys' tour; the most junior would do it. So Hamish it was. It transpired after a polite enquiry that he had kept once before, in an Under 15 'B' House match, so he was clearly better qualified than anyone else and no further discussion was required.

So with a broad grin and his ruddy cheeks redder than usual Big Dave led the troops out into the field. I settled back into my deckchair eagerly anticipating some further fun. But, no, something was wrong. Dave was running, well waddling quickly, back to the pavilion. Panic!

He had no umpire. The batsmen had covered during the first innings and as Bridgetown had supplied the one proper official Dave was morally obliged to provide the other. He came straight to me. 'Nigel, you wouldn't be kind enough to umpire for us, would you?' 'Yes, happily, Dave,' and then suddenly thinking ahead, 'but on one condition.' 'Oh, I'll certainly buy you a pint afterwards.' 'No, no,' I retorted, 'on condition you bowl my end!' Dave chuckled. 'Oh ... OK.'

And so, I was guaranteed a grandstand view of what promised to be the highlight of the tour.

It wasn't long before Bridgetown were well behind the clock. Nimmers had opened with as usual a tidy spell of off cutters and Scotty's left-arm spin was difficult to score off. At 53 for three after an hour it was time to open the game up. Cometh the hour ...

The Big Man peeled off and handed me his sweater. 'Right-arm over' he said to save me asking and put his mark down some six paces back. He then took an inordinate time getting his field right, but I have to admit he knew his stuff: deep square on the boundary, a man at 45, mid-wicket, mid on and, probably wisely, someone at cow corner ten yards in; and an orthodox off side with, ambitiously, a slip.

The first ball, a full-toss, was dispatched into the river. The kids probably anticipating some action had been ready and fished it out remarkably quickly, but not before the inevitable comments rained in. 'Wouldn't it be better if I stood in the river?' from deep square; 'what about all of us on the leg?' from cover. Dave was unmoved.

The second ball required me to stretch my arms out again, this time horizontally, as the ball pitching half way down the wicket and turning sharply bounced three times before being stopped by the slip well to his right. 'I can see why I'm needed here,' laughed Jabba. Dave was not amused, merely commenting as he passed me that at least the ball was turning. Correct, Dave.

The third ball was only four, going first bounce into the field behind us. The fourth received similar treatment but nearly got a wicket as it only just cleared the man at cow corner. The fifth brought the youths back into action with their net and the sixth saw a rather good shot as a comparatively good ball was cut gloriously past cover for four. The final ball of the over, remarkably, was a dot. In attempting to hit the biggest six yet the batsmen slipped and was very nearly bowled. This completely fooled Hamish who flapped at it and a bye resulted. 26 off the over. Could have been worse.

His second over conceded just 12, and Dave was in a far happier frame of mind when I handed back his sweater. 'I can feel it coming,' he said, 'the fingers are much more supple now.' I merely observed that I thought the batsmen were looking more relaxed too. The same could not be said of his own troops, though, as their initial mirth at their captain's attempt to bowl was already beginning to wear thin. Luckily there were still plenty of runs to play with.

It was the final ball of the third over that did it. 15 had come from the five balls and I think even Dave was about to concede defeat and take himself off. But the sixth was a beauty. It was the second attempt at a googly (the first had failed to land until it dropped out of the branches of the tree in the field behind us) and it pitched on a length on the off stump, went between bat and pad and hit leg. Dave leapt into the air, no mean feat in itself, yelling 'Yeeesss!'. The fielders yelled their delight, or perhaps surprise, and ran to celebrate with the Big Man, who judging from his awkwardness was quite unaware that 'high fives' were required for all. 'I knew he couldn't spot it,' he chortled.

A fourth over was now inevitable and it was a surprisingly good one. Three authentic leg-breaks pitching roughly in the right place were watched very carefully by the new bat and left alone. The flipper ... well, Dave said it was; it looked like a straight one to me ... hit him too high so I had to turn down the vehement appeal. Then two long hops. One went for four and the other sailed straight to deep square on the boundary, who caught it with ease. 'Bowling for that,' said the Big Man nonchalantly, whilst accepting the plaudits from his bemused teammates.

Bridgetown, being a typical village side, had no intention of shutting up shop, even if they knew how. The new batsman gave the charge to the first ball of Dave's next over, missed the shortish leg-break with a mighty swing of the bat and Hamish had time to fumble the ball, make an unholy mess of the stumps and still have him stumped with time to spare. The team were not slow to point out that their inspirational Leader was now on a hat-trick. But it was too much for the Mighty Man as he unleashed his faster ball which hurtled down the legside for four byes which I deemed to be wides as poor Hamish had no chance. Dave was most upset as he said they would now count against him. I politely suggested that the runs against column could absorb them without being noticed.

Success, I suspect, was beginning to go to his head and that together with an element of tiredness, as this just had to be the longest spell of his career by far, meant the rest of that over cost 10 more runs.

Luckily the dénouement was not long in coming, and the Deputy Headmaster was spared the ignominy of having to take himself off. Two wickets fell the other end, followed by a run out at the start of Dave's next over, doubtless caused by the determination of the one decent bat remaining to get up to the receiving end. He was hopelessly beaten by a direct hit from Coxy at cover. The no. 11, a callow youth of uncertain age, was no match for such a seasoned spinner on top of his game. He played and missed at four then got a leading edge that spooned gently back to the bowler who could claim his fourth victim and more importantly the kudos of leading the Saracens to their second victory of the week. He led his troops up the hill to the pavilion with his head held high, a broad grin stretching from ear to ear across a complexion that by now was almost puce, acknowledging the plaudits of all and sundry.

I'm not sure his final bowling figures were ever publicly revealed, but no-one, least of all himself, forgot the four wickets. Luckily it was the end of the tour and everyone needed to hit the road north or east so we were spared any regaling in the bar of how it was all done. Suffice it to say, the Big Man has not been invited to lead the troops again since this famous occasion, but he was subsequently awarded the Order of the Wine Glass (the one that holds a whole bottle) at the next mid-tour BBQ in honour of this, his greatest day.

11. CAPE TOWN

In those dim and distant days of the fifties an ordinary cricketer, schoolboy or adult, didn't think about playing abroad. I suppose some especially affluent and well organised people did manage to go and watch Test Matches abroad but it must have involved lengthy and expensive trips. It started to change, slowly, from the sixties onwards but nowadays it is the norm. My two sons each had a cricket tour from Shrewsbury, Ben to Barbados and Tom to South Africa; and our daughter Lucy had a lacrosse trip to the U.S. from Marlborough. When I arrived as Headmaster at Horris Hill in 1996 I was surprised to discover they had already had one cricket tour to Barbados and were in the throes of planning a second. Two to South Africa followed. How parents afford it, I often wonder, but as I know to my own cost there is an expectation from both school and child on the parent to cough up. Most schools now organise sporting trips abroad, and travel specialists offer a whole selection of possibilities to follow England whenever they are touring. And great fun they all are too, but I do think that that expectation from the school can be too great.

Personally I never had the good fortune to play on foreign fields and my first vested interest as a spectator was as a parent on Tom's tour in December 2000. Even then my responsibilities at home meant I could join in only after the first week, but I did witness what proved to be unquestionably the two best and most remarkable days of the whole trip.

A two-day/four-team tournament had been organised over a weekend by St Augustine's C.C., in Cape Town. I didn't know anything about this remarkable club in advance but it was not long before I found out. In the bleak days of apartheid it stood out as a beacon of hope in the battle for multi-racial cricket. This was the club where Basil D'Oliviera first came to prominence and more recently it has been the home club of Paul Adams, the left-arm spinner with the impossible contortion of an action who represented his country no less than 45 times. Their ground, a slightly barren, windy and sandy expanse, is to be found beside Princess Vlei (lake) in Heathfield just west of the M5, which is the vague boundary between the lush southern suburbs like Constantia and the realism for the majority of Capetonians of the townships. The ground may appear at first sight as a bit bleak by English expectations, but is lovingly cared for and produces a good cricket wicket. Since that first visit it has been gradually improved and it is now proudly called The Basil D'Oliviera Sports & Recreation Centre, officially opened by the great man himself.

The club had gone to town for this tournament with sponsorship, live coverage from the local radio station, and in typical South African style, various stalls had been set up to sell all sorts of goodies, not least food, and the distinctive aroma of braais (barbecues) pervaded the ground on our arrival. The local team had put out their Under 18 XI, as had the other invitees from Paarl C.C. and Gugulethu, a township team. The games were 30 overs a side, with bowlers restricted to a maximum of six. The draw meant Shrewsbury watched the morning game before taking on Gugulethu in the afternoon. I was particularly pleased as Tom had been chosen to take his turn as captain for these two days.

The morning game was exciting with St Augustine's just managing to scrape home in the final over. Shrewsbury batted first in the afternoon and scored a respectable 161 for nine with most batsmen contributing. Gugulethu looked a remarkably capable side and with plenty of wristy strokes and straight hitting were on for a comfortable victory until a disagreement over a call led to their best batsman being run out. The fall out from this led to three more quick wickets and suddenly Shrewsbury were back in the game. Tom managed his bowling changes well, giving all the spinners a go as it was clear Gugulethu were happier against speed. Some fine bowling and fielding under pressure just saw Shrewsbury home by five runs, with the last two wickets falling in the 30th over.

The reward was a welcome lie-in for the lads on the Sunday morning, the first of the tour, as the final was scheduled for the Sunday afternoon. We arrived just in time to see Paarl clinch third place, scoring the winning run off their penultimate ball. In the final Tom lost the toss and Shrewsbury were asked to bat. Again, contributions from all the batsmen led to a presentable score of 147 being set. St Augustine's willed on by a large and vocal crowd, crept closer and closer, sensibly keeping wickets intact. With 12 runs required off 18 balls and six wickets remaining they seemed to have the game within their grasp. This time a brilliant catch turned the tide – mid on sprinting back to clutch a skier. The pressure then started to tell and Shrewsbury kept the calmer. Two excellent run outs and a couple of other wickets, both to spinners, meant they won by three runs with St Augustine's 9 wickets down.

It had been a splendid tournament played in a tremendous spirit. All four games had gone to the final over and any one of the four sides could have won it. I suspect Shrewsbury did simply because they were better able to control their emotions at the death whereas the African sides all became a little excitable. But now it was time for the presentations African style. All the club officials had their say, and eventually the Chairman proudly presented Tom with the trophy. Then, horror of horrors, the poor chap was asked to say a few words in front of the gathered 500+ and the press! I don't know why I worried, he said all the right things, thanking all the right people and finally brought the house down and got the loudest round of applause and much cheering by concluding: "Finally, a special word of thanks to the ladies at Mama Kozi's, they're the best and biggest burgers I've ever had!" And this inevitably resulted in many hugs and kisses and photos in front of the relevant stall!

Tom receives the trophy from the Chairman of St Augustine's C.C.

*

On our very first visit to Cape Town, we were taken straight from the airport to Newlands cricket ground. There was a provincial game on that day, the only one during our week's stay, so it was then or not at all. We've all seen pictures of this famous ground, considered to be amongst the most attractive of all the Test grounds, but no picture can do justice

106

to the awesome presence of That Mountain. We sat on the grassy bank called The Oaks and just soaked in the view. We soon got used to the Castle Brewery and the regular rattle of the railway in the foreground, but couldn't get over the majesty of the vast slopes of verdant trees defying gravity, intermingled with outcrops of vertical, bare rock, all enhanced by the azure blue of the almost cloudless sky behind. It was simply stunning, and regular visits to the ground do nothing to diminish the effect. It is high on our list of places to take friends who visit, especially those keen on their sport.

Newlands
on our first visit, February 1999

In January 2003 we had two of Lucy's friends from Marlborough staying, Mike Roberts and Dave Geddes, both outstanding rugby players but neither were cricketers. When I suggested a trip to Newlands to see the first day of the South Africa v Pakistan Test, they both, being well brought up young men, said they'd very much like to come, they'd never been to a Test Match before. I suspect it was said with tongue in cheek but at least they'd get a view of the Newlands Rugby Ground next door, and this could be a fall back for a tour should the cricket become deadly boring. So along the five of us trooped hoping we'd get some decent entertainment ... at least Herschelle was playing.

Herschelle Gibbs is, to me, one of the superstars of world cricket. He is a true entertainer. His batting is explosive and his fielding panther-like; he is one of very few players who can raise the levels of anticipation and excitement before a game. Inevitably he can disappoint but I've lost count of the majestic innings of his that I've been lucky enough to witness in person. He's quite a character, even without the lurid tales of his private life, who has the nickname of scooter. Apparently this came about when as a 16 year old he made his debut for the then Western Province and couldn't get to training as he was too young to drive, so his team-mates suggested he got himself a scooter. I don't know to what extent he stills avails himself of this mode of transport, but we were going to see the great man play on this day.

Graeme Smith won the toss and chose to bat. He opened as usual with Herschelle and from the very first over you got the impression that Waqar Younis, the Pakistani captain and opening bowler, wasn't enamoured with the prospect of a day's fielding. Smith and Gibbs, on the other hand, were up for it and we were treated to what must be one of the more remarkable day's Test cricket of all time. The first wicket fell an hour or so after tea when the score was 368. This was Smith who was bowled for a modest 151 and only 18 fours. Gibbs remained for a further 45 minutes until he was caught with the score on 413. He had received 240 balls and scored 218 runs, including 29 fours and 6 sixes! The ground rose as one to acclaim him. It had been the most devastating annihilation of a Test attack. The remaining 10 overs of the day were inevitably a bit of an anticlimax but even so South Africa closed on 445 for three. They had scored at exactly 5 runs an over as 89 overs were bowled.

The three young Marlburians had been unable to take their eyes off the action throughout the day, and they weren't alone in that. 'Test cricket is a bit better than I thought!' said Mike.

*

9th February, 2009

One of the advantages of spending six months in South Africa each year is the sport on tele. Last night Supersport 1 had on live the domestic 20/20 semi-final deciding match of three, between the Warriors (Port Elizabeth) and the Eagles (Bloemfontein); Supersport 2 had the Dolphins (Durban) v Cobras (Cape Town) semi-final decider at the same time and Supersport 6 had West Indies v England Day 4 from Antigua. It was interesting moving from the Test to the frantic 20/20. Give me a Test

Match any day but if proof were needed, last night showed why 20/20 fills the grounds, and that must be a good thing.

There is a lot at stake in the 20/20s. The finalists will play for R700,000 (R500,000 to the winners) a figure that pales into insignificance in comparison to the R5 million each finalist will get simply for qualifying for the Champions League in India as the South African representatives. We are keen that the Eagles win their game as they finished 4th in the table so if the Cobras, our home team, can win, the final will be played at Newlands.

The Eagles win the toss and insert the Warriors entirely due to the fact that rain is about. Despite being hot favourites the Warriors are bowled out for 97.

Meanwhile in Durban, the game we mostly watch, the Cobras win the toss and bat. Herschelle Gibbs dances down the wicket third ball to Jayasuriya and is easily stumped. Graeme Smith and JP Duminy, with no little difficulty, take the score to 60 odd in about 9/10 overs before Smith very unluckily drags a ball outside the leg stump back on to it. Enter Justin Ontong, right-hand bat, who has played for South Africa and is a useful all-rounder. He scores 30 odd in 20 balls including one cover drive for four off Jayasuriya when he takes guard as a left-hander. Never seen that before! Duminy holds the innings together and the Cobras finish on 148 for four, which the pundits reckon is a winning total given the conditions.

Back in PE the Eagles are making heavy weather of reaching their modest target and are going along at about 4 an over but are regularly losing wickets. Boeta Dippenaar their captain is still there though.

In Durban Jayasuriya plays outside the line to Charl Langeveldt's first ball of the innings which swings in to him. Plumb LBW! One run later H.M. Ackerman, their other big striker, hooks firmly but uppishly and is brilliantly caught one handed at square leg. Dolphins 1 for two in the first over which soon becomes 11 for three. Game over? Hashim Amla though is looking ominously good and Johan Louw another big hitter (who earlier in the season against the Cobras with six needed to win the match off the last ball did just that!) is playing rather too sensibly and the score mounts remorselessly. Around 80 after about 12 overs, so only just under the rate, Amla is brilliantly caught in the covers and we heave a sigh of relief. In comes Smit, the very promising young wicket-keeper … who also bowled three very good overs of leg-spin! … and he nudges and nicks several boundaries. It's getting tight again.

On the screen flashes the news that Dippenaar is out. Change channel. Eagles need 16 off 2 overs, four wickets left.

Back to Durban. Claude Henderson the veteran left-armer has been brought back, turns his first ball sharply and has Smit stumped, and four balls later has the elder Amla removed the same way. Dolphins 126 for six with two overs to go, but Langeveldt to bowl the 19th.

Back in PE the Eagles need 8 off the final over, 3 wickets left.

Langeveldt bowls a (mostly) brilliant over only conceding five runs ... one a wide ... and one an overthrow when he himself hurls the ball at an already broken wicket with no-one near to gather ... and takes two wickets. Dolphins need 18 off the last to win. We must be home and dry.

In PE the Eagles have lost a wicket, but scored six, so need two off the last ball.

In Durban Vernon Philander is to bowl. A talented but wild and unreliable all rounder. It shows. We have a wide, two fours, two singles and a dot. Six needed off the last ball to tie. Johan Louw facing.

In PE the Eagles drive firmly to cover. Brilliantly stopped and returned. One run only. Match tied.

I shout at Philander to get it in the blockhole or at least a low full-toss. He must have heard! Low full-toss! Perfect. Except Louw removes it into the upper tier of the stand on the longest boundary. An unbelievable strike. Match tied.

Have both semi-finals in the same competition ever been tied before? And both at almost exactly the same moment!

*

In the meantime, several thousand miles further west, England have declared and Gayle and Devon Smith are calmly eating away at the 500 target.

*

Confusion reigns in both PE and Durban. Warriors think they have won. Cobras can't believe it. Commentators talk about a bowl out. Luckily the umpires are on the ball. The rules state there is to be a one over play off. The side who has just batted, bats first and nominates any three batsmen. The fielding side nominates any one bowler. Normal fielding restrictions. If two wickets fall the innings is finished. Both grounds are still packed. No-one can bear to leave. We give up on PE and concentrate on Durban.

Langeveldt is the chosen bowler. Total confidence in him. Best in the business at the death. First ball: Jayasuriya steps outside his off-stump and plays one of his trademark, flamboyant hooks for six. Except that he misses and loses his leg-stump. In comes Smit. Interesting choice. Second ball down the leg. Wide. Third ball carved through the covers. Superbly stopped on the boundary by Duminy. Two runs. Fourth ball one run. Louw now facing. Tremendous swing at fifth ball. Top edge. Disappears into the night. Eventually comes down and is caught. Dophins 4 and out. Cobras have 5 to win. Chosen batsmen Gibbs, Smith and Duminy. Fancy our chances! After what seems an extraordinarily long interval Gibbs drives the first ball to extra cover and sets off as does Smith the non-striker. But Jayasuriya flings himself at the ball and somehow with only one stump to aim at throws down the wicket at the bowler's end with Smith hopelessly adrift. 0 for one. Gibbs late cuts for 2 down to third man and then with all the fielders in a circle steps down the wicket and lifts it over extra for 4.

In PE it was straightforward. The Eagles scored a challenging 14 and then got the two wickets in three balls. So the Final is at Newlands! On Saturday evening ... and it will be packed ... but it can't possibly be anything like this!

(It wasn't. But to the joy of the partisan crowd, the Cobras won the trophy.)

*

Of all the many changes and developments in the game today, I find the advent of modern technology one of the most fascinating. This was brought home to me a couple of years ago sitting on the upper deck of the pavilion at Newlands. I was with Martin Foster, the wicket-keeping friend from Felsted days and we were watching the MTN 40 over day/night contest between the Cape Cobras and the Highveld Lions. I had tempted him along particularly as the great Herschelle would be playing so we were assured of some sparkling entertainment. Herschelle inevitably was out first ball. (Two weeks later I took another friend along on the same pretext. Herschelle drove the first ball of the innings imperiously through the covers and I nudged David and said "There you are. Half an hour of that will keep you happy!" Of course, he was out next ball!)

Whilst watching the Lions match, Martin was on the phone to his son James, who was somewhere in central India on the England 'A' Tour lying on his hotel bed watching cricket, none other than the Cobras v Lions game from Cape Town! In the middle of the phone call there was an incident with Andrew Puttick, the Cobras opening bat who at this point in time was keeping wicket as he often does in limited overs games. We couldn't see clearly what had happened. He seemed to fumble the ball then belatedly broke the wicket and yelled an appeal for a stumping. The umpires referred the matter to the TV official, and of course as a spectator you simply have to wait, often an agonisingly long time, for adjudication to be made. In the meantime James, from the depths of the Deccan, was able to tell us exactly what occurred. 'Awkward ball down the leg-side, off the pad, did well to stop it but dropped it, missed the stumps at the first attempt, but didn't have the ball, gathered the ball and broke the stumps with the batsman just out. Brilliant effort for a part-time keeper.' About two minutes later in Cape Town this news, which by now was old hat to us experts, was broken to the participants and the rest of the crowd.

From a television point of view that incident was doubtless straightforward when viewed two or three times, but would have had to have been given not out otherwise. The human eye cannot cope with the speed involved but all straight-line decisions like run outs are now clear to everyone. The development of Hawk-Eye is especially fascinating as dependant on how much you wish to trust the technology you are moving from an opinion of the umpires into a factual decision. It amazes me how often the umpires are proved to be correct in their decision making, and in fact the technology is showing just how good most of these umpires are. I particularly admired the development used in the 2009-10 South Africa v England series which brought in zones of certainty/uncertainty for any LBW referral. What this meant was that the on-field umpire's decision stood unless Hawk-Eye proved it to be completely erroneous. If, for example, a not out referral showed the ball would have clipped the outside of the stumps, the decision stood as the ball was in the 'zone of uncertainty'; had it been shown to be hitting middle, the referral would have been upheld as it was 'certain' to have hit the stumps. Again, the umpires were largely proved to be correct. I also liked the fact that referrals were reduced to two per side per innings, which meant the captains used them more judiciously. I'm all for umpires retaining their autonomy, but everyone, umpires included, want as many decisions as possible to be correct, and to be seen to be correct, and technology is making that possible. I hope it can be extended to be used in all Test matches throughout the world as quickly as possible as it is here to stay, especially with the technology improving all the time as we saw in the 2010/11 Ashes series.

12. OVER AND OUT

One of the fixtures each year at Felsted was against the XL Club, to qualify for which you have to be aged forty or over. They were a friendly bunch, always played the game the right way and invariably the side contained one or two who had played first-class cricket. Their batting was always strong, the bowling a bit weak but the fielding at times bordered on the embarrassing. I determined there and then I would never let myself get into such a position and that I'd stop playing sooner rather than too late. In fact increasing responsibilities at Summer Fields meant that I had to stop playing regularly in 1979, but I still played the occasional Thursday and Sunday game until I first became a Headmaster in 1988. From then on it was only holiday games in Devon, which became increasingly pleasurable as Ben and Tom started to get involved. I don't think it crossed my mind to stop altogether until nature took its course and the sign was too clear to be ignored.

It was the late 1990s, and as usual North Devon entertained a variety of touring sides at their picturesque ground in Instow. Each week there would be three or four home games and John Edwards and the other team managers were hard pressed to raise full XIs for every game without falling back on holidaymakers and schoolboys. Well into my fifties by now, I wouldn't volunteer my services but would help out in dire need. Such was this occasion in mid-July, our first week of the summer holiday, against, I remember, the Sou'westers, a thoroughly competent wandering side from the home counties, captained by my old friend from those schoolboy games at Lord's, Philip Spray.

It was a glorious summer's day, not too hot, a pleasant breeze off the sea and there were several familiar faces in the North Devon side so all was set fair for a good day out. John was skippering and on the basis that our bowling could never defend a score but our batting might chase one successfully, elected to field upon winning the toss. The first part of his argument looked pretty sound as the visitors raced to 263 for five before declaring very fairly around half-time. If the North Devon bowling was weak, our fielding was unusually presentable in the face of the onslaught and even the distinguished shape of Canon (recently elevated to such lofty status) Henry Pearson was seen to leap a full inch towards the heavens in an attempt to pluck a catch out of the air. Sadly it just clipped the top of his finger and on returning to terra firma, he reduced us all to fits with his apology: "The spirit is willing, but I'm sorry – the Good Lord didn't bless me with a figure for ascension!"

The chase was given a solid base by the Aussie pro and two first teamers, but a flurry of wickets meant I was required to do a bit more than I really felt capable of when I joined the good Canon at the crease with the score 181 for six just after the start of the final 20 overs. I was greeted by a young wicket-keeper hidden behind his helmet with the comment "Blimey, which museum did you borrow that bat from?" Years of experience had taught me not to get involved in any banter, but I was a bit thrown by this. I looked down at my bat, which looked perfectly normal to me, and said "What's wrong with it?" "Granpa, that Gray-Nicolls tape went out with the ark. And I'd get a helmet on if I were you, the quickie's coming back next over." I politely pointed out that I'd never ever worn a helmet and had no intention of starting now. My hackles were up so I defiantly played a forward defence of perfection personified to the one remaining ball of the over and strode up the wicket for counselling from the padre.

Poor Henry was still recovering from the two threes the somewhat younger previous partner had made him run, and suggested we built our partnership on sensible singles and boundaries if and when possible. "With our combined ages, Nigel, we simply won't last if we have to do too much running." I was in total agreement, and slowly but surely the score mounted without either of us taking any risks or running any threes. We were, however, getting a bit behind the rate to the extent that with ten overs left we still needed another 55. At this point Philip cunningly changed tactics and brought back the spinners which meant we were going to have to hit the ball to get our runs rather than just guide and place it as we had been doing. Several fielders were strategically placed on the boundary so inevitably our running had to increase too. In the next three overs we managed to add 18, but we'd had to run the lot and our puffing and red faces told their own tales.

It's on occasions like these that the Instow ground and the North Devon club come into their own. It was a beautiful summer's evening, the sun just beginning to sink towards the western horizon and to cast its reflection over Lundy and Bideford Bay. The tide was in and the waters of the Taw/Torridge estuary were lapping contentedly against the sea wall at the edge of the ground. Plenty of members were starting to crowd outside the delightful old thatched pavilion, pints in their hands, egging us aged gentlemen on to do the club proud and provide a victory.

Even the President had got out of his car to witness the dénouement. 37 required off 7 overs.

To the first ball of the next over, I stepped down the wicket to the off-spinner and struck him over his head, one bounce into the pavilion wall. A great burst of applause greeted our fifty partnership, but it was beneath the dignity of the Canon and the Head to touch gloves or show any such modern symbol of camaradie. We were too exhausted anyway! And then it happened. An off-drive way into the deep and Henry bellowed "TWO" as he shot off the mark; I sped to the other end, turned and saw it was going to be close as the fielder gathered the ball. I set off on the second and immediately felt a sharp arrow pierce the back of my right thigh. I hobbled onwards to the middle of the wicket as the ball reached that wretched keeper on the second bounce, and with a great flourish he whipped the bails off and yelled the unnecessary appeal. I could hardly move, and with a lengthy and the most undignified exit imaginable, I left the field of play, as it transpired for the very last time in a proper game of cricket. I'd torn my hamstring which ended any chance of playing again that year, which in turn told me enough was enough.

Sadly, Henry was out the following over – ever the humorist, he said he'd come out in sympathy. The last two wickets fell soon after and we lost by 20 odd runs. But it had been a good game, and, injury aside, the greatest fun.

*

One of the privileges of the Headmaster of Horris Hill was to oversee the annual Arabs Match. This fixture had started way back in 1947 when E.W. Swanton brought his famous, and then quite young, club to play Monty Stow (the then Headmaster)'s XI on the picturesque school ground. It became quite a feature of the calendar and in the days when the boys were rarely allowed home, it became an occasion when parents could come and see their sons and they would picnic around the field while watching the game. Over the years a number of distinguished cricketers graced the occasion, and The Great Man would say a few appropriate words at tea and present bats to the two leading school players of the year. R.M. Stow's XI became M.J.L. Stow's when Jimmy took over the reins and it was still thus when I arrived, although Jimmy required, understandably, increasing help to raise a team of suitable strength of Old Boys and other acquaintances of the school. My first Arabs Match in the summer of 1997 was the 50th Anniversary, but sadly it had to be called off due to rain. Head-magisterial duty required that

The picturesque ground at Horris Hill

we entertained the Swantons and Stows to lunch. It was a thoroughly jovial occasion, but The Great Man refused to call me Nigel, or even Chapman; it was a very formal 'Headmaster' throughout! It was tempting to recall the incidents of yesteryear but discretion was the better form of valour and I resisted. His life in the circles of the great and the good of the cricketing universe guaranteed he would not have recalled my previous insignificant appearance on his radar. Afterwards he planted a tree on behalf of the Arabs to commemorate the occasion but little else was possible. The following year had a similar lunch, and a good game of cricket, but it was his final visit as he died in January 1999. The game that year understandably failed to materialise, and it was with some difficulty that we got the one in 2000 off the ground. It proved to be the last ever fixture.

With the help of Mark Smith, the master i/c, I raised the team for this game. We managed to get several competent Old Boys, including two from the Radley team that year, as well as three connections from Shrewsbury, my elder son Ben, and two who were Gap students at Horris Hill, Rob Hillman and Nimmers, Rob Champion. So it was quite a youthful side and it was important they had a wise and inspirational leader to cope with such a powerful opposition. So I rang Johnny Barclay, who had preached brilliantly in one of our Chapel Services and therefore I felt he was qualified to play! He said he'd be delighted. And he all but won us the match off his own bat.

The Arabs, as ever, were very strong but Johnny manipulated his bowlers with the cunning of the old pro and the young responded to his encouragement and belief. Nick Phillips from Radley with 8 overs for 9 runs and Nimmers, another seamer, 6 for 7 were the pick of the six bowlers Johnny used which, sadly, didn't include himself. But for an explosive innings from Trevor Webster, who had played a number of times for the Transvaal in the mid-nineties, the Arabs would have struggled. From 123 for five they put on 69 in 9 overs of which Trevor contributed 55 and they were able to declare on 192 for five. Sadly his contribution didn't end there as he followed that up with 7-36 in 16 overs, bowling at a formidable pace not at all pleasant for the young especially on a prep school wicket that was inevitably a bit too lively with such a bowler. The only people who coped were Mark Smith who batted extremely well for 41, and the captain. Johnny went to the crease when the score was 120 for six and 15 overs left. He had the situation under control at once. A single here, a two there, a boundary an over, he scored off almost every ball he faced, and the total, and excitement, mounted as the impossible became tantalisingly within reach. It was a masterly cameo of how to bat under pressure, and it was just a pity he hadn't put himself in earlier. But that would not have been him, and, as he said, not the point with so many youngsters deserving of a go before him. He was the last man out for 32 when we were on 167, just 25 short. At least there was no Colonel to remove him on this occasion! Instead, he died a valiant death being caught in the deep off Trevor Webster but still remonstrated with himself for getting out with the game there for the taking.

It was appropriate that a long-running and well-known fixture should come to an end with such a distinguished cricketer nobly trying to win the day; and how ironic that it should be a Summer Fieldian attempting to rescue Horris Hill!

*

I should have loved to have played in that game, but it was a fanciful dream – even ten years earlier I would have struggled. I still made one annual appearance and that was for the Common Room side in the 20 overs game against our friends and neighbours from Cheam School, but in 2001 it became obvious even that was stupid, even dangerous. It was not the batting – I made it quite clear I was no. 11 and woe betide the ninth member of the side to get out. Luckily I rarely had to get my pads on. On this occasion I recall I did and had a nervous couple of overs after the eighth wicket fell. No. 10, sensible man, remained undefeated and the archaic Gray-Nicolls could rest in peace.

I did, though, of course, have to field and the nature of these games is that everyone has to bowl two overs. This I quite enjoyed, and a day or so before the game I would appear in the school nets just to get the arm over and into the groove so I didn't make a complete fool of myself. On this occasion I surprised everyone, not least myself and especially the opposition, by taking three wickets for just five runs. The first was a useful wicket as the batsman concerned was scoring fast. I suspect he failed to realise just how slow the leg-break was, as he struck it with all his might, but far too early. It ascended to a considerable height, in fact they managed to run two in the meantime, before it came down straight into the safe hands of Nimmers who had to move barely a couple of yards to his right at deep mid off. I nonchalantly admitted to the junior staff that I had, of course, been bowling for that. Their respect for the Boss must have gone up even higher in the second over, when the new batsman completely misread the undisguised long-hop, which on this occasion, most unusually, failed to turn, kept a bit low and bowled him all ends up. This brought in the Cheam Head of Classics, Robert Romaines, doubtless an excellent teacher (unquestionably very well grounded as he'd been a boy at Horris Hill), and although a lover of the game of cricket, not a performer of note. Doubtless, he'd been told I bowled leg-spin and being an intelligent person he would have had a clear idea of what to expect. Cricket, as we all know is a game largely played in the mind, so bringing to bear on the moment all my years of experience, decided to give Robert the high lob with just a tweak of the googly on it. The poor chap was completely thrown by this grenade appearing out of the sky, took a couple of strides down the track, swung his bat wildly at thin air, slipped over with the effort and lack of spikes, and was lying prone in the middle of the wicket as the ball landed roughly on a length and turned sweetly to hit middle and off. It was highly entertaining and even their umpire was roaring with laughter as he handed me my sweater.

All would have been marvellous had it ended there. But two overs later, fielding at short extra cover, with a man either side way behind in the deep to save me any running, their Aussie gap, no mean cricketer at all, smashed a ball straight at me at head height. I saw it all the way, realised instantly it was a catch, moved my head inside the line and shot my right hand up to try and clasp it. In reality my hand must have moved barely at all by the time I felt a whoosh of air millimetres from my right ear. As the ball careered over the boundary bisecting the deep fielders, I thought: 'Jesus ... but for the grace of God. This is dangerous.' I knew what to do, all the right instincts were there ... but I couldn't do it, in fact couldn't get anywhere near. It was time to call it a day.

As ever, Cheam were excellent hosts and we had a wonderful supper with the beer and wine flowing. Mark Johnson, their charismatic Head, whom I knew well from our days teaching together at Summer Fields, mercifully kept his speech shorter than usual which meant, in turn, my words of gratitude could be equally brief. We boarded the minibus in a very happy frame of mind – this wonderful game of cricket had been a winner yet again.

*

So anno domini meant that I gradually, and for the most part gracefully, retreated from the field of play into the pavilion to observe and inevitably pass comment on the antics of the modern cricketer and the way the game is now played. Us 'Golden Oldies' are obviously always right and the game can never be as good as it was in 'My Day'. The trouble is we look at it with a jaundiced eye and it's fruitless to compare different eras. Times have moved on and we just have to accept that the game is different. Today's youth will find exactly the same in thirty or forty years time in much the same way as our elders must have been appalled at our antics thirty or forty years ago.

At Felsted in the sixties there was a bachelor who regularly came to umpire school games as indeed he did in the cricket week at the end of term. He was a chap called Basil Hunt who was well known in amateur cricketing circles in Essex and reluctant as we boys were to admit it, he was actually quite a good umpire. But he was a stickler for correct behaviour and the right etiquette on the cricket field. That was the way he was brought up and he was not going to change now. In the sixties, of course, strictures on behaviour and familiarity were beginning to ease, Christian names were becoming the norm, you were starting to say what you thought rather than politely keeping it to yourself, and, as they always do, the youth of the day were pushing the boundaries as to how far they could go. There were two contrasting and, in their different ways, amusing incidents with Basil which epitomised the conflicting eras.

It was a chilly day, and Doug Smith who opened the school bowling and had already given Basil two long-sleeved sweaters, now peeled off his short-sleeved one and handed it to him.

"Smith. I am NOT a clothes-horse."

There was a pregnant pause as they looked each other up and down. Doug, we all knew, could be relied upon to say what he thought.

"Oh, Basil, I thought you were!"

You could almost see the smoke issuing forth from Basil's stout frame, as he hauled himself up to his full height.

"You will kindly refer to me as Mr Hunt. And you can remove these sweaters to the pavilion."

The second occasion involved myself whilst batting during a game after the end of term. On the last ball of the over I was hit on the pad and we ran a leg-bye. Basil walked off towards square leg to take up position for the next over. I was preparing to face and as the bowler was running in, he suddenly stopped. The mid-wicket was shouting " You're out!" I didn't know what was going on but when I turned towards him I could see Basil's finger was up and he said: "You're out LBW."

"You can't give me out LB from square leg!"

"I can. It was the last ball of the last over."

"But over has been called, so it's too late."

"But the next ball has not been bowled, so you're out."

"But nobody's appealed. You can't give me out just like that."

"The mid-wicket appealed as he passed me. So you're out. Now off you go."

As you can imagine, I was furious and went past him loudly muttering about ancient umpires not knowing the Laws.

At the lunch interval Basil sought me out, the latest edition of Wisden in his hands open at the appropriate pages.

"I can understand you were very upset, so I will ignore what you said. But if you look here you will see I was within my rights."

And he was. I had to hand it to him. The aged are not always as out of touch as they may seem.

As it turned out it was a useful incident. I've quoted it on many an occasion, often asking the boys at school how can you be given out LBW from square leg!

*

I often wonder how much the modern professional, and especially the game's administrators, appreciate they are in the entertainment business. If you and I didn't go and watch, what would be the point of it all?

And we all go to be entertained. One day cricket is still understandably popular (although I for one wish the powers that be would settle on either the 50 over format, or the 40 over one, and stick to it worldwide for one day competitions), but the real upsurge in interest in the game in recent years has been due to the arrival of the 20/20 competitions in their different guises. The grounds are packed for instant gratification and the entertainment is often spectacular. It is all cleverly packaged and presented and it is bringing a lot of money into the game as well as spectators who would not normally want to watch cricket. With the one concern that there is a danger of overdoing it, there is no doubt that the administrators have got this aspect of the game right, and the players have adapted superbly to the different skills required, to make it a splendid spectacle.

But what is happening to the longer format of the game? There will always be, one hopes, a place for Test cricket, although it is a worry that too many Tests around the world are played in front of all but empty grounds. But for Test cricket to remain viable, it in turn has to be fed by competitive domestic competitions of three or, better, four day duration. In England this has always been the County Championship which, no matter how the authorities tamper with it, rarely attracts any crowds of note which must be dispiriting for the players and financially can hardly be justifiable. The problem, I suspect, is to do with the entrenched traditions of eighteen different counties, none of whom, understandably in the light of their loyal members, wishes to give way to any imaginative ideas to modernize the competition that might see their own position compromised. But who are we trying to serve here? Each individual county? Or Test cricket and the England team in particular? As the large majority of the income for cricket is derived directly or indirectly from Test cricket it is pretty obvious what the answer should be.

Eighteen counties playing a championship, in no matter how many divisions, in front of a few members is, and someone needs to say it, plainly ridiculous. There has to be a competition to ensure the continuance of Test cricket. But, why can't there be, say, eight or nine teams, call them regions, franchises, or double-up counties, what you will, playing a midweek four day championship with home and away fixtures taking up most but not all of the weeks of the season. Then at the weekends you could revert to the eighteen counties and have the 50 over league competition on Saturdays, and a 20/20 one on Sundays. There would still be space on spare days or in spare weeks to fit in some knock-out competitions. All the counties would thereby retain their identity, but would no longer have to prop up a non-viable championship. Any change along these lines would inevitably lead to a higher standard competition and considerably reduce running costs. I cannot imagine it would increase attendances by any huge amount, but it just might. I do not pretend that there would not be many problems that would have to be sorted before such a dramatic revolution to the established order could get off the ground, but it seems to me to be a more imaginative way forward than continuing with the status quo. Wishful thinking, no doubt!

Not that this is necessarily a recommendation, but in South Africa they have reduced all the domestic competitions to six franchises and it seems to work. They do have different issues to cope with, but the talent is undoubtedly much more concentrated and thanks to a seemingly flexible transfer system, the franchises are reasonably evenly balanced. It has taken a few years for supporters to identify with the new groupings but they now seem firmly established. All the grounds attract large attendances for the limited over competitions, but there is little interest in the four day format. Indeed at Newlands there is no charge to attend the latter but even so hardly anyone watches.

The longer format of the game is a difficult product to sell anywhere, but in England it would be a better product if there were fewer games of higher quality.

*

Cricket has given me an enormous amount of fun both as a player and a coach, and now as a spectator, and I hope will continue to do so for many more years. I was lucky to have had enough talent briefly to come into contact with some well known players and to play on some famous grounds, but looking back the greatest enjoyment has come from being involved with the young and from trying to transmit my love of the game to them. Their enthusiasm for the game is unquenchable and infectious and is the real reason I feel the same about the game now as I did all those years ago when dear old EWE instilled a love of the game in all his charges, of whom I was so lucky to be one. I just hope that some of those for whom I have been responsible over the years, will one day be able to look back and say the same.

INDEX

Ackerman, H.M.   109
Adams, Paul   104
Allen, Gubby   11, 18
Allom, Anthony   61
Altham, Harry   40, 48
Amla, Hashim   109, 110
Amos, Dave   95
Arnold, Geoff   50-53
Austin, Bill   24

Bailey, David   37, 40
Bailey, Trevor   49, 50, 54, 55
Barclay, John
    6, 11, 12, 65, 71, 116, 117
Barker, Andrew   38, 39, 61
Barker, Gordon
    35, 36, 49, 50, 68, 73
Bear, Michael   54
Benaud, Richie   99
Blofeld, Henry   64
Bodkin, Peter   65
Bowtell, Eric   75
Boyce, Keith   50, 53, 56-58
Brett, Oliver   13
Brocklehurst, Ben   59
Brooks, Freddie   24
Busby, Roger   77, 78

Carling, Phil   44, 45
Carruthers, Frank   24
Cass, Rodney   55
Champion, Rob (Nimmers)
    98, 101, 116-118
Chapman, Ben   19, 90-93,
    96-98, 104, 113, 116
Chapman, Charles   20, 23, 48
Chapman, Leslie
    20-26, 37, 48
Chapman, Lindsay   90
Chapman, Lucy   104, 107
Chapman, Mary
    20, 22, 23, 26, 27, 48

Chapman, Tom (Barn)
    90-96, 98, 100, 104-106, 113
Christy, Martin   61, 63
Close, Brian   54
Cockett, John   28, 29,
    32-37, 59, 60, 66, 68, 71
Corbett, Scott   98, 101
Cowdrey, Chris   64
Cowdrey, Colin   64
Cox, Tom   98, 103
Crabtree, Harry
    69, 70, 73, 74
Craig, Nick   45-48
Crossley, Alan   77, 78, 88

Daniels, Rupert   42-48
Dash, Terry   56, 57
Davey, Michael   24
Davis, Roger   44, 45
Debenham, Frank   24
Dickson, David   71
Dippenaar, Boeta   109
D'Oliveira, Basil   104, 105
Duminy, J.P.   109, 111
Dunbar, J.G.   37, 39, 42
Dunstan, Richard   36

Eardley, Lyn (EWE)
    9, 10, 44, 67, 122
East, Ray   52-54
Edmeades, Brian   41, 42, 54
Edmonds, Mike   44-48
Edwards, John
    90, 92-97, 113
Ekins, Tony   62, 63

Fletcher, Keith   56
Foster, James   111, 112
Foster, Martin
    6, 59, 60, 61, 63, 66, 111
Freeman, Lou   24, 25

Frewer, Lou   83
Furley, Nigel   78

Garner, Phil   88
Gear, Robert   92, 95
Geddes, Dave   107
Gibbs, Herschelle
    107-109, 111
Gibson, Trevor   77-79
Gilliatt, Richard   60
Goodwin, Paul   43, 45, 48
Gough, 'Mac'   27, 67, 74

Hahn, Stan   86
Hayes, Paul   80-82
Henchman, Robbie   16
Henderson, Claude   110
Higgins, Tim   32
Hillman, Rob   116
Hobbins, Graham   78
Hobbs, Robin   41, 42, 54
Hooper, Mike
    43, 45, 46, 48, 52, 53, 60
Hunt, Basil   119, 120
Hunter, Robert   29
Hutton, John   42, 45

Jackson, Ted   61-63
James, David   111
Jardine, Douglas   18
Jayasuriya, Sanath   109-111
Jeffries, Brian   88
Jesty, Trevor   48
Johnson, Graham   48
Johnson, Mark   119
Jorden, Tony   55

Keep, Jamie   59, 60
Knight, Barry   54-57
Knight, Nick   50, 66

Langeveldt, Charl   109, 110

Lawrence, Pat 40-42
Leaver, Peter 30
Lee, Martin 78
Lever, John 52
Lewis, Henry 59
Lindsey, Pete 42
Lloyd, Martin 78, 79
Louw, Johan 109-111
Luckin, Roger 27, 59, 60, 61, 63
Luckin, Sam 60, 66
Lurcock, Tony 81, 82

Maby, James 14
MacFarlane, Ian 82
Mackay, Richard (Jabba) 98, 100, 101
May, P. B. H., 60
McKenzie, Hamish 100-102
Mealing, Alf 24, 25
Morris, Peter 73
Moylan-Jones, Lt. R. 46
Mungre, Cpl. A. 46, 47

Nawab of Pataudi 18
Neale, Eric 81
Neate, Pat 42, 44, 45
Nichols, Jack 24, 25
Nokes, Roger 28, 30, 31, 61
Nurton, Mike 86-89
Nutting, Mike 31

Oliver, Richard 30, 31
Ontong, Justin 109

Parry, James 71
Pearson, Henry 92-94, 96, 113-115

Philander, Vernon 110
Phillips, Nick 117
Phillips, Ted 34
Pineo, Richard 75, 78
Polk, James 14
Popplewell, Oliver 62, 63
Porter, Simon 78, 83, 88
Pretzlik, Nick 39
Price, John 92
Pringle, Derek 50, 65, 66
Pritchard, Graham 53
Prodger, Peter 25
Puttick, Andrew 111

Quick, Arnold 40

Radley, Clive 41
Rice, Algy 61, 63
Ridley, Giles 88
Rist, Frank 26, 49-55, 68, 74
Roberts, Mike 107, 108
Robertson, Jack 40
Romaines, Robert 118
Roope, Graham 39, 43, 45-48
Rushton, Roger 92, 94, 96

Savage, Pat 75
Saville, Graham 41, 54
Sayers, Denis 42
Shackleton, Derek 86, 87
Sharp, Harry 43
Silcock, Freddie 24, 25
Smit, Daryn 109-111
Smith, Doug 30, 32, 33, 37-39, 60, 61, 119, 120
Smith, Graeme 108, 109, 111

Smith, Mark 116, 117
Smith, Peter 83-86, 88
Smith, Ray 28, 29, 31, 37, 38, 67, 68
Snell, Chris 10-12, 67
Spray, Philip 43-46, 48, 113, 114
Stackpole, Keith 58
Stapleton, John 78
Steele, David 38
Stephenson, John 50, 66
Steward, Tony 42
Stow, Jimmy 115
Swanton, E. W. 47, 48, 58, 115, 116

Taylor, Brian 56, 57
Taylor, Derek 53
Thicknesse, John 32
Tolchard, Roger 43-48
Trueman, Fred 54, 55

Wait, Oliver 35, 36
Walker, Dave 98-103
Waller, Bob 25
Webster, Trevor 117
Whitby, Lew 25, 26
Williams, Capt. D. 46, 47
Williams, Nicko 65, 98
Winlaw, Tony 59
Winstone, Robin 83
Winther, David 12-17

Yeabsley, Doug 88
Younis, Waqar 108

125

Life Beyond the Airing Cupboard
John Barclay

MCC & Cricket Society Book of the Year 2008

A lovely read, self-deprecating and full of gentle humour.
Simon Barnes, *The Times*

Like all good books about sport, it is about more than that;
it is about life, love and loss, too.
Mike Atherton, *The Times*

These moving reflections on cricket and life glow with a winning
generosity of spirit, soaring above petty rivalries to approach,
at times, the level of spiritual meditation.
Paul Coupar, *The Wisden Cricketer*

Small format hardback, b&w illustrations, 240 pages, £15

Now I'm 62
The diary of an ageing cricketer
Stephen Chalke

The cricket market is so full with ghosted autobiographies and books
designed to be read on the toilet. It is a rare thing to find a work
of such originality and quality as this.
Andy Bull, *The Wisden Cricketer*

I loved it. There was something to savour on every page.
I really laughed – so much that my wife thought I'd gone mad.
When I was nearing the end, I slowed down my reading,
not wanting it to finish.
John Barclay

I thought it was a wonderful read. Beautifully written.
I was drawn completely to its emotional honesty.
Several passages were dark, much darker than I expected;
Others made me laugh out loud. I couldn't get enough of it.
Simon Lister, *cricket author*

Softback, b&w illustrations, 208 pages, £12

Fairfield Books, 17 George's Road, Bath BA1 6EY
telephone 01225-335813